THE MOUNT VERNON
LADIES' ASSOCIATION WAS FOUNDED IN 1853.
THE ASSOCIATION PURCHASED MOUNT VERNON IN 1858 FROM
JOHN AUGUSTINE WASHINGTON, A GREAT-GRANDNEPHEW OF
GEORGE WASHINGTON, AND HOLDS THE PROPERTY UNDER A CHARTER
FROM THE COMMONWEALTH OF VIRGINIA. ITS MEMBERS ARE CHOSEN
TO REPRESENT THE SEVERAL STATES AND SERVE WITHOUT SALARY.
THE ASSOCIATION WAS THE FIRST NATIONAL HISTORIC
PRESERVATION ORGANIZATION IN THE UNITED STATES.

THE OBJECT OF THE MOUNT VERNON LADIES' ASSOCIATION SHALL BE:

*To perpetuate the sacred memory of "The Father of his Country"
and, with loving hands, to guard and protect the hallowed spot
where rest his mortal remains.
To forever hold, manage and preserve the estate,
properties and relics at Mount Vernon,
belonging to the Association, and, under proper regulations,
to open the same to the inspection of all who love
the cause of liberty and revere the name of
Washington.*

THE OFFICIAL BADGE OF OFFICE OF
THE VICE REGENTS OF THE MOUNT VERNON LADIES' ASSOCIATION.

A BRIEF HISTORY OF THE ASSOCIATION IS DESCRIBED INSIDE.

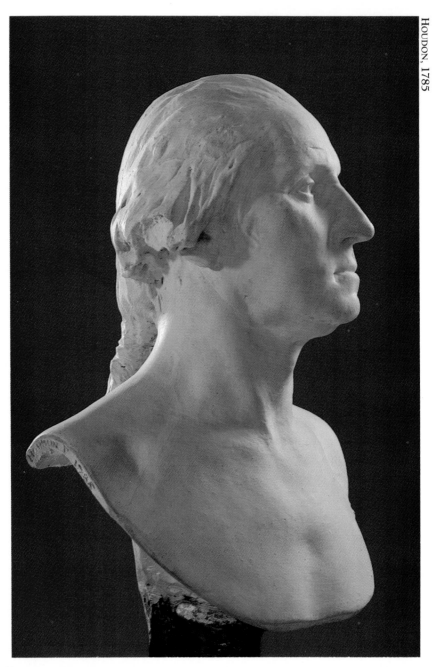

FIRST IN WAR, FIRST IN PEACE, AND FIRST IN THE HEARTS OF HIS COUNTRYMEN,
HE WAS SECOND TO NONE IN THE HUMBLE AND ENDEARING SCENES OF PRIVATE LIFE.

—HENRY LEE, DECEMBER 26, 1799

MOUNT VERNON

A HANDBOOK

THE MOUNT VERNON LADIES' ASSOCIATION
OF THE UNION, MOUNT VERNON, VIRGINIA

www.mountvernon.org

GEORGE WASHINGTON'S BOOKPLATE,
ENGRAVED FOR HIM IN LONDON IN 1772,
INCORPORATED THE WASHINGTON FAMILY COAT-OF-ARMS.

COPYRIGHT © 1974, 1985, 1998 BY
THE MOUNT VERNON LADIES' ASSOCIATION
TEXT: CHARLES C. WALL, CHRISTINE MEADOWS,
JOHN H. RHODEHAMEL, ELLEN MCCALLISTER CLARK
1998 EDITION TEXT: MICHAEL C. QUINN
DESIGNED AND PRODUCED: COGNOSCENTI
1998 EDITION DESIGN: MBL STUDIOS
TAYLOR LEWIS PHOTOGRAPHS COPYRIGHT © 1985 BY TAYLOR LEWIS
ADDITIONAL PHOTOGRAPHY:
PAUL KENNEDY: COVER, PAGES 8, 9, 10, 14, 15, 111, 26-27, 63,
86 BOTTOM LEFT, 136, 137
TED VAUGHAN: PAGES 18, 58, 73, 125
HARRY CONNOLY: 45, 46 TOP, 68, 70-71, 77, 79, 84-85, 86 TOP,
106, 109,132, 133 TOP, 90, 92-93, 96
CAROL HIGHSMITH: PAGES 20, 24-25, 120, 125
HOWARD MARLER: PAGE 142
RICHARD AND JUDITH WHITMORE: PAGES 35 UPPER LEFT AND RIGHT,
37, 40-43, 66 BOTTOM, 67 BOTTOM.
DEAN NORTON: 23 TOP, 113, 116
RUSS FINLEY: PAGE 121
JOE COMICK: PAGE 128
WILLIAM K. GEIGER: PAGES 127, 129
ED OWENS: PAGES 140, 141 BOTTOM
OTHER PHOTOGRAPHS: MOUNT VERNON LADIES' ASSOCIATION

THE WASHINGTON FAMILY

BY EDWARD SAVAGE—1796

The artist has portrayed General and Mrs. Washington with their two wards, George Washington Parke Custis and Eleanor Parke Custis, grandchildren of Martha Washington by her first marriage. In the background a servant in the red-and-buff Washington livery waits in attendance. The map, to which Mrs. Washington points with her fan, is of the "Capital City," then being developed on the banks of the Potomac. Savage made copper plate engravings of this painting in 1798, four of which were purchased by General Washington. One of these originals may be seen in the small dining room. THE NATIONAL GALLERY OF ART, ANDREW W. MELLON COLLECTION

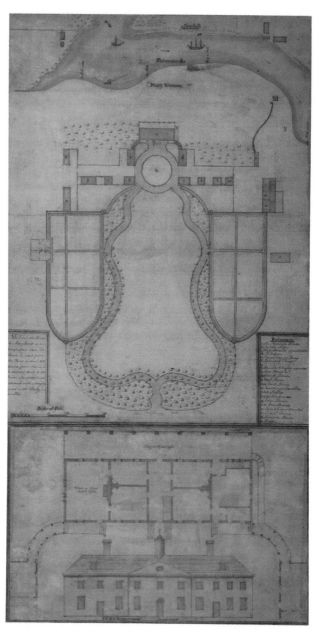

THE VAUGHAN PLAN OF MOUNT VERNON, PRESENTED TO GEN-
ERAL WASHINGTON BY SAMUEL VAUGHAN IN NOVEMBER 1787.
THE PLAN IS BASED ON NOTES MADE BY VAUGHAN IN JUNE OF THAT
YEAR, AND ITS ACCURACY IS ATTESTED BY GENERAL WASHING-
TON'S LETTER OF ACKNOWLEDGMENT.

CONTENTS

A BRIEF WASHINGTON– MOUNT VERNON CHRONOLOGY

1674	John Washington, great-grandfather of George, is granted the Mount Vernon homesite.
1726	Augustine Washington, father of George, acquires the Mount Vernon property from his sister, Mildred.
1732	George, first child of Augustine and Mary (Ball) Washington, born at the family place on the Potomac River in Westmoreland County, Virginia.
1735–39	Augustine Washington in residence at Mount Vernon with his young family.
1743	Augustine Washington dies. Lawrence Washington, George's elder half brother, marries and settles at Mount Vernon.
1752	Lawrence Washington dies at Mount Vernon.
1754	George Washington acquires Mount Vernon by lease from Lawrence Washington's widow.
1759	George Washington marries Martha Dandridge Custis, widow of Daniel Parke Custis, and settles at Mount Vernon with his wife and two young stepchildren, John Parke and Martha Parke Custis.

Martha Washington

1761	Inherits Mount Vernon following the death of Lawrence Washington's widow.
1775	Elected General to command all Continental forces.
1781	Stops briefly at Mount Vernon en route to and from Yorktown. John Parke Custis dies; the Washingtons take in his two youngest children, Eleanor Parke and George Washington Parke Custis.
1783	Resigns his commission to Congress and retires to Mount Vernon.
1787	Presides over the Constitutional Convention in Philadelphia.
1789–97	Years of the presidency. Visits Mount Vernon fifteen times.
1799	Dies and is entombed in the old family vault.
1802	Martha Washington dies and is entombed beside her husband. Mount Vernon passes to Washington's nephew Bushrod Washington.
1829	Bushrod Washington dies, leaving Mount Vernon to his nephew John Augustine Washington.
1853	Mount Vernon Ladies' Association founded by Ann Pamela Cunningham of South Carolina to purchase and preserve the home and tomb of George Washington.
1858	Mount Vernon Ladies' Association receives its final charter from the Commonwealth of Virginia and purchases Mount Vernon from John A. Washington, Jr.

A BRIEF HISTORICAL PREFACE

No estate in United America is more pleasantly situated than this. It lies in a high, dry and healthy Country 300 miles by water from the Sea, . . . on one of the finest Rivers in the world. . . . It is situated in a latitude between the extremes of heat and cold, and is the same distance by land and water, with good roads and the best navigation [to and] from the Federal City, Alexandria and George town; distant from the first twelve, from the second nine, and from the last sixteen miles.

Time and circumstance have wrought no changes to qualify or invalidate the foregoing description of Mount Vernon from a letter written by George Washington to an English correspondent in 1793. Mount Vernon stands as a monument to its builder, *pleasantly situated* on a commanding eminence, overlooking the Potomac and the low Maryland hills. The tree-crowned hilltop, the wide sweep of the river, and the wooded shores beyond present a prospect of unchanged beauty.

The rivers of Virginia were broad avenues offering easy access to a rich interior, and their shores were rapidly settled after the first precarious years in the history of the colony. George Washington's great-grandfather, John Washington, was a pioneer settler of the Northern Neck (the area between the Potomac and the Rappahannock rivers). This ancestor, the emigrant, established himself along the lower Potomac in Westmoreland County about 1657. In 1674, John Washington and Nicholas Spencer were granted five thousand acres of land along the upper Potomac, between Dogue and Little Hunting creeks, by Thomas, Lord Culpeper, proprietor of the Northern Neck under dispensation of his patron, King Charles II. The grantees were obliged to pay an annual quit rent in perpetuity and "to seat and plant" the land within three years. In 1690, the tract was divided between Lawrence, son of John Washington, and the heirs of Nicholas

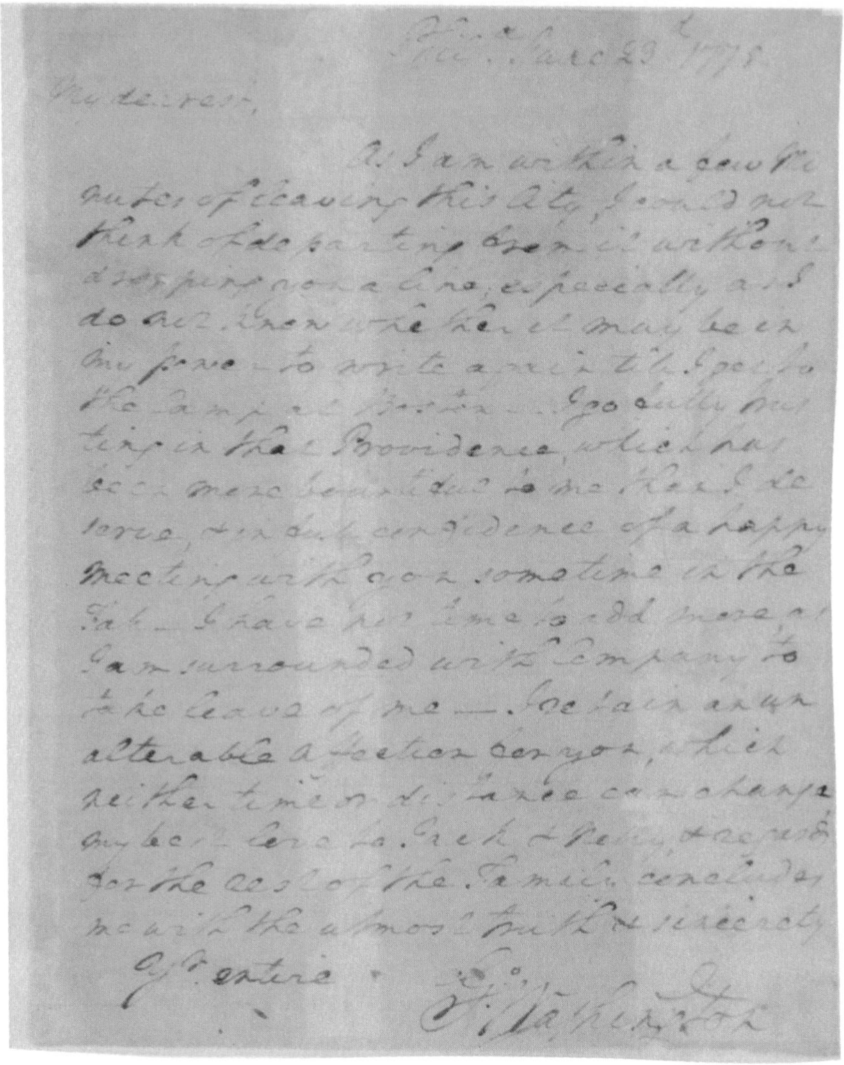

Phil^a., June 23^d., 1775

My dearest,

    As I am within a few Minutes of leaving this City, I could
not think of departing from it without dropping you a line, especially
as I do not know whether it may be in my power to write again till
I get to the Camp at Boston—I go fully trusting in that Providence
which has been more bountiful to me than I deserve, & in full
confidence of a happy meeting with you sometime in the Fall—I
have not time to add more, as I am surrounded with Company to
take leave of me—I retain an unalterable affection for you, which
neither time or distance can change my best love to Jack & Nelly,
& regards for the rest of the Family concludes me with the utmost
truth & sincerity

Y^r. entire G^o: Washington

Spencer. From Lawrence, the Washington half of the grant, then known as Hunting Creek Plantation, passed to a daughter, Mildred. In 1726 Augustine Washington, father of George, purchased the Little Hunting Creek Plantation from his sister, Mildred, and her husband, Roger Gregory. In 1735, when George Washington was three years old, Augustine removed his family from their plantation on Pope's Creek (now officially designated Washington's birthplace) in Westmoreland County to the Hunting Creek Plantation. Four years later he moved once again, establishing his household at the Ferry Farm, on the Rappahannock River near Fredericksburg.

In 1740 Augustine Washington deeded the Little Hunting Creek Plantation to his son Lawrence, who had just come of age. By the time of his marriage in 1743, Lawrence had settled on the estate and had renamed it in honor of Admiral Edward Vernon, under whom he had served in the Caribbean. Augustine Washington died in 1743, and his young son George spent a part of his youth with his elder half brother at Mount Vernon. In 1752, Lawrence died, and two years later George Washington came into possession of Mount Vernon by purchase of the life interest of his brother's widow. When she died in 1761, Washington inherited the estate.

The history of this early period is poorly recorded. It must be drawn or deduced principally from wills, title papers, and archaeological evidence. It was not known until the first vestry book of Truro Parish was discovered, about the turn of this century, that George Washington's father had resided at Mount Vernon. In the absence of this information, it had been assumed that the central portion of the present house was built by Lawrence Washington in 1743. The vestry book revealed that Augustine Washington was a vestryman of Truro Parish, in which Mount Vernon is situated, in 1735 and for several years thereafter. Supplementary evidence, since brought to light, establishes the fact that he resided at Mount Vernon from 1735 until 1739. It is also recorded that Lawrence Washington's inheritance included a "patrimonial Mansion." The survival of this early structure within the fabric of the present house is confirmed by a diarist, who in 1801 identified the central portion of the house as having been "constructed by the General's father."

From 1752 until 1759, George Washington's military service, as aide to General Braddock and as commander of Virginia militia, permitted only infrequent visits to Mount Vernon. During this period the plantation was managed by his younger brother, John Augustine. Fort Duquesne fell in November 1758, and George Washington retired to private life. In January

---

FACING PAGE: SHORTLY BEFORE HER DEATH, MARTHA WASHINGTON DESTROYED HER CORRESPONDENCE WITH HER HUSBAND; ONLY TWO LETTERS OF GEORGE TO MARTHA, EITHER OVERLOOKED OR DELIBERATELY SPARED, ARE KNOWN TO SURVIVE. BOTH DATE FROM THE PERIOD IMMEDIATELY FOLLOWING WASHINGTON'S APPOINTMENT AS COMMANDER-IN-CHIEF OF THE CONTINENTAL ARMY IN JUNE OF 1775. THE LETTER SHOWN HERE, ONE OF THE GREAT TREASURES OF THE MOUNT VERNON MANUSCRIPT COLLECTION, WAS WRITTEN JUST MOMENTS BEFORE GENERAL WASHINGTON SET OUT ON A JOURNEY THAT WOULD LEAD THROUGH PERIL TO VICTORY AND A SHINING PLACE IN HISTORY.

PAINTING OF THE EAST FRONT OF THE MANSION WITH NORTH LANE OUTBUILDINGS,
ATTRIBUTED TO EDWARD SAVAGE, *CIRCA* 1792

1759, he married Martha Dandridge Custis, widow of Daniel Parke Custis. To an English friend he wrote, *I am now, I believe, fixed at this Seat with an agreeable Consort for Life and hope to find more happiness in retirement than I ever experienced amidst a wide and bustling World.* This expectation of retirement was to be disappointed, but the peaceful years together at Mount Vernon before the Revolutionary War were the happiest of their lives. There is an echo of this in the lines George Washington wrote to his wife from Philadelphia in 1775, on the eve of his departure for New England as newly appointed Commander-in-Chief of the Continental Army: *I should enjoy more real happiness in one month with you at home than I have the most distant prospect of finding abroad, if my stay were to be seven times seven years.*

During the war years Martha Washington spent eight winters with her husband in his northern encampments, from the first at Cambridge to the last at Newburgh, leaving Mount Vernon in the late autumn and returning in the spring as the opening guns announced a new military campaign. George Washington stopped briefly at Mount Vernon en route to and from Yorktown in 1781. Lund Washington, distant cousin and faithful friend, managed the estate in his absence. General Washington resigned his commission at Annapolis in December 1783, and returned to Mount Vernon. Once again he looked forward to the life of a private citizen and husbandman on the bank of the Potomac, but again he was disappointed. He remained at Mount Vernon until he assumed the presidency in 1789, but

14

COMPANION VIEW OF THE WEST FRONT
WITH A FAMILY GROUP ON THE BOWLING GREEN

his fame and inevitable position as leader in the movement for a stronger union denied him the domestic ease he desired.

In the eight years of his presidency, George Washington visited Mount Vernon fifteen times, remaining for periods that varied from several days to several months. On his retirement in March 1797, he returned home once again and, in the two and one-half years that remained to him, he enjoyed a greater degree of the tranquillity he had so long desired. He died on December 14, 1799. Mrs. Washington survived until May 1802.

In the forty-five years of George Washington's tenure Mount Vernon grew in size from 2,126 acres to approximately eight thousand. By the terms of his will, this estate was divided after the death of Mrs. Washington. The Mansion and four thousand acres were inherited by Washington's nephew Bushrod, while the rest of the estate passed to other heirs. From Bushrod Washington, Mount Vernon ultimately descended to John Augustine Washington, Jr., a great-grandnephew of General Washington, who conveyed the property to the Mount Vernon Ladies' Association in 1858.

On this rout you traverse a considerable wood, and after having passed over two hills, you discover a country house of an elegant and majestic simplicity.

J. P. Brissot de Warville, 1788

THE MANSION GROUNDS

George Washington referred to the area around his home as the *Mansion House Farm*, but it was not a farm in the usual sense of the word. There were no field crops, big barns or large herds of cattle or sheep near the Mansion. Instead Washington developed this area of about five hundred acres as an American version of a gentleman's country seat. While he carefully laid it out to be gracious and beautiful, he also ensured that it served many practical purposes for his plantation enterprises.

The design for the buildings and grounds around the Mansion is entirely George Washington's concept. He developed much of the plan before the Revolutionary War, relying on his practiced surveyor's eye and drawing ideas from an influential gardening book, <u>New Principles of Gardening</u>, by Batty Langley, that he acquired in 1758. Langley introduced a rural, naturalistic design, which were features that Washington knew and appreciated from growing up in Virginia and his years on the western frontier.

THE COLONNADE TO THE KITCHEN

FACING PAGE: LOCUST TREES IN THE GROVE NORTH OF THE MANSION

THE MANSION FROM THE WEST GATE

Washington began rearranging the outbuildings around the Mansion before the Revolution and never let work come to a full halt, despite his 8-1/2 year absence and wartime shortages and disruptions. When Washington returned to Mount Vernon at the end of the Revolution, he energetically carried his plan for the grounds to completion. By the time he finished, around 1789, he had replaced every outbuilding, relocated lanes and roads, leveled and expanded lawns, and re-shaped Mount Vernon's gardens.

The new plan created a majestic setting for the Mansion. The grounds closest to the Mansion resembled a park, with groves of trees, walled gardens, and broad lawns leading either to open pastures or to a border of deep woods. Looking east or west, visitors enjoyed striking vistas. To the north and south, Washington arranged outbuildings neatly along lanes. Ever practical, Washington's scheme separated the work areas of the plantation from the leisure ones, yet kept both close to the Mansion. The master of Mount Vernon was as likely to be supervising work in the outbuildings as he was to be proudly showing a guest his gardens and groves.

View of the North Lane

George Washington's love of trees is revealed in his writings about the Mansion's grounds. Writing from his military headquarters in New York in August of 1776, he directed his farm manager: *[plant]...groves of Trees at each end of the dwelling house,...these Trees to be Planted without any order or regularity (but pretty thick, as they can at any time be thin'd) and to consist that at the North end, of locusts altogether, and that at the South, of all the clever kinds of Trees (especially flowering ones) that can be got.*

Ten years later, as he supervised the grading of the bowling green lawn on the west side of the Mansion, Washington filled his diary with references to the young trees and shrubs that he selected to be planted here. Around the lawn, he laid out two graceful, serpentine walks, which were to be shaded by tulip poplars, white ash, and elm. Several of the larger trees on

Road to my Mill Swamp ... and to other places in search of the sort of Trees I shall want for my Walks, groves and Wildernesses.

Diary of George Washington, January 12, 1785

the bowling green are originals, planted under Washington's direction in 1785. He enthusiastically created "Wildernesses," along the serpentine walks, naturalistic plantings filled with native shrubs and saplings. To complete the view from the Mansion, Washington cut and pruned trees in the outlying woods, opening a view to Mount Vernon's west entrance gate, a half-mile away.

Washington capitalized on the sweeping panorama of the Potomac by planting trees on the hill that slopes down to the river. These trees were carefully pruned to frame the magnificent view rather than block it, creating a much-admired "hanging wood."

Today, the view across the Potomac River is an active part of the preservation of Mount Vernon. Starting in the 1940s, the Mount Vernon Ladies' Association has led a campaign to protect the pristine appearance of the Maryland shore. Congresswoman Frances P. Bolton, who served as Vice Regent for Ohio from 1938 to 1977, launched the effort by purchasing 750 acres of land to save it from development. Through Mrs. Bolton's generosity, this tract became the nucleus of Piscataway National Park, a four-thousand acre preserve of federal and private land, created by an act of Congress in 1974. The adjoining private property is governed by deed restrictions that ensure that new development is low-scale and sensitively designed to preserve the view from Mount Vernon and the natural woodlands of the shore.

George Washington created a formal courtyard on the west front of the Mansion. At the center of the courtyard is a large circle–really an ellipse, carefully laid out with Washington's surveying skill. The circle had the practical function of enabling horse-drawn carriages to bring guests and travelers directly to Mount Vernon's door, and then easily turn around and retire to the stable. The 32 posts around the circle, which correspond to points of the compass, and the chains between them are restorations of original features. Washington's diary includes an entry that he sent a wagon *with the Posts for the Oval in my Court Yard, to be turned by a Mr. Ellis at the Turng. Mill on Pohick.* His cash account contains a record of the exact number of posts turned and ornamental drops carved and the cost of the work. In the center of the circle is a post, just as there was in Washington's time, bearing a sundial, now a replica of the original.

George Washington carefully separated the grounds around the Mansion from the surrounding fields with a sophisticated system of sunken walls, gardens and fences. The sunken walls, called ha-ha walls, are designed to be unnoticed in the view from the Mansion, yet keep cattle, pigs and horses from the Mansion's groomed lawns. By closing four gates in the evening, the formal grounds and gardens of the Mansion House Farm were effectively protected from hungry wildlife and grazing livestock.

I have no objection to any sober or orderly person's gratifying their curiosity in viewing the buildings, Gardens &ct about Mount Vernon.

George Washington to William Pearce, November 23, 1794

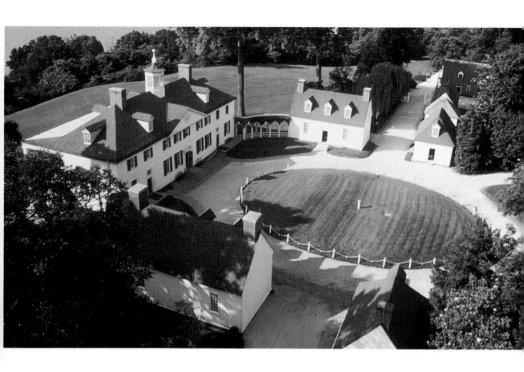

THE COURTYARD IN FRONT OF THE MANSION.

THE HA-HA WALL PROTECTING THE MANSION'S EAST LAWN.

23

THE SERVANTS' HALL

The first building entered on the tour is a one and one-half story outbuilding, on the left side of the Mansion. It dates from the first phase of Washington's reconstruction of the grounds, when he was absent during the opening years of the Revolution. Washington's manager at the time, a relative named Lund Washington, at first misunderstood the purpose of the new building, thinking it was to house a laundry, as had the previous building on the site. By the time Washington's correction reached Lund, an oversized fireplace, adequate to heat large kettles of water for washing, was already in place.

The large fireplace remained, but other aspects of the building plan were revised, making it a handsome and impressive accommodation for the servants of visitors. These personal servants, valets, maids, and coachmen were both slaves and hired servants of the dignitaries and landowners who visited. The building was put to other uses as well, becoming a dwelling for a newly-hired farm manager and his family in the 1790s during Washington's presidency. In the inventory taken immediately after Washington's death, the servants' hall was sparsely furnished, containing only andirons, half a dozen fire buckets, two small linen cupboards, a pair of simple walnut tables and six folding "camp" seats.

THE MANSION

The will of George Washington's grandfather, Lawrence Washington, probated in 1698, reveals that tenants were then living at the Little Hunting Creek Plantation, later to be known as Mount Vernon. Their place of habitation is not known, but there is evidence of an earlier house in the basement walls of the present structure. The Mount Vernon cornerstone, removed from a cellar wall for better preservation and now displayed in the museum, bears the initials L. W. and a curious design, suggestive of the seventeenth century, but it is undated and cannot be definitely assigned to Lawrence, the grandfather of George. George also had a half brother named Lawrence, who preceded him as proprietor of Mount Vernon. In the absence of more definite evidence, this first chapter in the history of Mount Vernon cannot be completely reported, although the available facts suggest

that a tenant house, or quarter, was built on the site of the present Mansion by George Washington's grandfather.

The dwelling acquired by George Washington after the death of his elder half brother was of modest size and typical of its locality and period. It was one and one-half stories high with a central hall and four small rooms on the first floor. (Drawings of the conjectured evolution of the Mansion are to be found on page 125.) This nucleus of the present structure had been built by Augustine Washington, who resided here on his Hunting Creek Plantation for several years in the 1730s with his second wife, Mary Ball, and their young family, the eldest of whom was George.

In 1759, Mount Vernon acquired a mistress, and the master's correspondence for the preceding period of several years records the enlargement of his modest villa in anticipation of the event. The house was raised from one and one-half to two and one-half stories and was extensively redecorated. While the work was in progress, George Washington was absent on military duty, and the builder was supervised by a neighbor,

27

William Fairfax of Belvoir, an adjoining estate. Correspondence with Fairfax and others records the progress of improvements. Invoices of the period list the hardware and tools necessary to such a project, all of which had to be imported from the mother country. This pre–Revolutionary War house had its dependencies, gardens, and planted areas. The outbuildings were fewer in number and smaller; the gardens were less extensive than they now are. No ground plan or comprehensive description of the country seat at this stage in its development has survived. An entry in the master's diary reveals that the house had four principal dependencies, and that they were connected to the main house by "Pallisades" on low brick walls.

In 1773, George Washington made plans for additions to each end of the "Great house" and ordered materials from England. In July of the following summer he wrote to a friend, *I am very much engaged in raising one of the additions to my house, which I think (perhaps it is fancy) goes on better whilst I am present, than in my absence from the workmen.* These additions were part of a larger plan, which contemplated replacement of existing outbuildings with larger structures, creation of service lanes, development of the bowling green, and enlargement of the formal gardens. In May 1775, before the interior of the first Mansion addition was finished, George Washington departed to attend the Second Continental Congress in Philadelphia. There he was commissioned Commander-in-Chief of the Continental Army, and, except for brief visits en route to and from Yorktown in 1781, he was away for more than eight years.

MANSION AND COLONNADE FROM THE NORTH

DETAIL OF THE PALLADIAN WINDOW

In the absence of General Washington, his manager and distant kinsman, Lund Washington, continued the improvements already begun. Under his supervision the addition to the north end of the Mansion was raised and enclosed. The wing buildings and connecting colonnades were built. Forty-seven of Lund Washington's wartime letters to his employer form a valued part of the Association's manuscript collection; they record the progress of his work and his varied problems. On one occasion a British man-of-war appeared off Mount Vernon and demanded provisions. Lund met their demands, and the property was spared, although twenty slaves were carried away. On learning of this incident General Washington wrote to Lund:

I am very sorry to hear of your loss; I am a little sorry to hear of my own; but that which gives me most concern, is, that you should go on board the enemys Vessel, and furnish them with refreshments. It would have been a less painful circumstance to me, to have heard, that in consequence of your noncompliance with their request, they had burnt my House, and laid the Plantation in ruins. You ought to have considered yourself as my representative, and should have reflected on the bad example of communicating with the enemy, and making a voluntary offer of refreshments to them with a view to prevent a conflagration.

General Washington surrendered his commission to Congress, sitting at Annapolis, in December 1783, and turning homeward with two of his former military aides, reached Mount Vernon on Christmas Eve. Much remained to be done to the Mansion before it would be completed to the state in which the visitor now sees it, but little was accomplished in 1784. Public affairs still claimed his attention. In the autumn of 1784, General Lafayette visited Mount Vernon and is said to have been entertained in the unfinished *New Room*. Lund Washington's wartime accounts indicate that the piazza was erected in 1777, but there was a delay in finding stone flagging for the pavement. Suitable stone was imported from England and laid in 1786. The final embellishment of the house, a weather vane for the cupola, was not added until the autumn of 1787. Appropriately enough, it features the dove of peace.

Mount Vernon is an outstanding example of colonial architecture. It has much in common with other houses of the period, yet is unique in many ways. It owes its charm more to harmony of composition than to the beauty of its component parts. It has been assumed that George Washington had assistance in designing his home, and efforts have been made to identify his architect, but the assumption is not supported by the record. Architecture was not an established profession in his day, and there is no evidence in his correspondence or in his domestic records and accounts that he sought or received architectural guidance. The influence of the Governor's Palace at Williamsburg is apparent at Mount Vernon in the proportions of the wing buildings and in the bowling green, which corresponds to the palace green. Numerous similarities to other contemporary houses might be identified, but there is nothing to indicate that they were more than coincidences of style or common antecedent. General Washington had access to eighteenth-century English books on the design of country houses; the Palladian window and other details of the house, both exterior and interior, were copied or derived from one or another of these books. Here his skilled workmen may have been intermediaries since the books were written for the use of master builders. Many artisans were employed at Mount Vernon, but their work was limited in scope. It is apparent that, through the long years of development, overall planning was the province as well as an important occupation of the master. That he also supervised in some detail is indicated by the comment of a guest who

THE MANSION FROM THE EAST LAWN. CALL BELLS, USED TO SUMMON THE SERVANTS, WERE LOCATED AT THE SOUTH END OF THE HOUSE NEAR THE KITCHEN.

observed, "It's astonishing with what niceness he directs everything in the building way, condescending even to measure the things himself, that all may be perfectly uniform."

The most striking architectural feature of the Mansion is the high-columned piazza, extending the full length of the house, a splendid adaptation of design to setting and climate. It seems to have been a complete innovation and would, in itself, entitle George Washington to distinction among architects.

The exterior finish of the Mansion and of the courtyard dependencies is another unusual feature. The siding was beveled to give an appearance of stone; sand was then applied to the freshly painted surface. This treatment, called *rusticated Boards* by Washington, pre-dates the Revolutionary War and was used elsewhere in Virginia, but no precedent has been found for such extensive use.

The interior of the Mansion reflects architectural decoration popular from 1757 when Washington first enlarged his father's house to his last addition completed in 1787. Paint colors changed with the fashion and those now seen in the house reproduce the colors favored by Washington at the end of his life. A scientific analysis of all interior painted surfaces established a complete chromochronology from the second half of the eighteenth century to modern times. Physical evidence revealed in this study is corroborated by Washington's surviving orders for dry pigments. Wherever possible, eighteenth-century formulas and techniques of application were used in the restoration to achieve the proper period effect. Round brushes, like the kind used in Washington's time, were imported from France for the restoration, and pigments were hand ground and mixed on the estate. Where the evidence called for wallpaper, original fragments were examined microscopically and the fibers matched to English wallpapers with similar fiber construction. The paper was then applied in rectangles of approximately twenty-one by twenty-eight inches with slightly overlapping horizontal seams to simulate the appearance of eighteenth-century wallpaper. It was not until the nineteenth century that rolls of wallpaper were made in a continuous sheet.

Mansion room settings are based on a 1799 inventory prepared after George Washington's death. This fifty-page document lists the contents of each room with appraised values of every item. The appraisers were remarkably thorough, listing the subject or title of each print and painting and the title of every book, map, and pamphlet. Livestock, tools, and equipment were included for each of the five farms that comprised the Mount Vernon estate. A similar inventory, compiled in 1802 following Martha Washington's death, indicates only minor changes in furnishings during the two and one-half years of her widowhood. These basic documents are augmented by orders, invoices, correspondence, wills, early descriptions of the Mansion, and other domestic records. Because of Washington's lifelong habit of preserving his papers and the care given them by his heirs, it is safe to say that Mount Vernon is the best documented historic house for its period in the country.

THE LARGE DINING ROOM

This two-story room is most frequently designated in General Washington's writings as *the large dining room*, and occasionally as *the New Room* because it was the last addition to the house. The wing of which it is the principal part was raised and enclosed by Lund Washington, manager during the Revolutionary War. In 1776, while threatened by the British army and by the dwindling of his own military resources, General Washington found time to write from Harlem Heights to Lund of his plans for this room in the following words:

The chimney of the new room should be exactly in the middle of it—the doors and every thing else to be exactly answereable and uniform—in short I would have the whole executed in a masterly manner.

The room interior remained unfinished until the end of the war and for several years thereafter, while the master of Mount Vernon sought a craftsman who could execute the decoration of ceiling and woodwork in a manner equal to his expectations. His correspondence on the subject has been correlated with surviving physical evidence to form the basis of the present decoration. His inquiries express a preference for plain wallpaper, green or blue, with harmonizing border. The present wallpaper border was reproduced from fragments of the original, and the two shades of vertigris green are documented as the original colors. From Philadelphia in 1787, he directed that the woodwork of the room be painted a *buff inclining to white*, which might later be changed. This letter and physical evidence have determined the woodwork colors as now restored. The doors and those elsewhere on the first floor are believed to have received their "mahogany" finish in 1797 when the pine woodwork in the principal passages was grained or painted to simulate a more costly wood.

In January 1799, a young English guest noted "white chintz window curtains with deep festoons of green satin" in this room. Martha Washington identified the white material as dimity in her will. The present draping of the windows, incorporating satin and dimity of proper color and weave, follows the fashion of the period. The young guest also reported that there was "an East Indian mat" on the floor. This testimony is corroborated by an inventory, which was prepared for the General's executors early the following year.

DETAIL OF APPLIED PLASTER DECORATION ON THE PALLADIAN WINDOW WAS EXECUTED IN 1786 WHEN WASHINGTON COMPLETED THE INTERIOR OF THE LARGE DINING ROOM.

The mantel was the gift of Samuel Vaughan, an English admirer and friend of General Washington. It arrived in 1785, as the decoration of the room was in progress. The mantel vases were also presented by Vaughan and are of English manufacture. They were made about 1770 at the Worcester factory. The decoration is the work of Jefferyes Hamett O'Neale.

Outstanding among the furnishings of this room is the pair of Hepplewhite sideboards. To the right of the Palladian window is the surviving mate of a pair made by John Aitken of Philadelphia in 1797. The matching sideboard is another Aitken piece, but has no association with Mount Vernon. Beneath the Palladian window are nine of the original twenty-four Aitken chairs made for this room.

Two eighteenth-century landscape painters are represented by the four large oils, personally selected by Washington. The rather somber views of the Great Falls and the Potomac River at Harper's Ferry, West

I have the honor to inform you that the chimney-piece is arrived, and, by the number of cases (ten) too elegant and costly by far, I fear for my own room and republican style of living.

George Washington to Samuel Vaughan, February 5, 1785

THE GREAT FALLS OF THE POTOMAC BY GEORGE BECK, 1796

Virginia, were painted by George Beck. The river scenes above the interior doors are the work of William Winstanley in 1793. The inventory, compiled after George Washington's death, lists twenty-one paintings and engravings in this room, including the representation of Louis XVI, the Trumbull engravings of the death of General Montgomery and the battle of Bunker's Hill, and the moonlight scene over the mantel.

Although identified by Washington as a dining room, this handsome space was used for a variety of functions. The absence from the inventory of a formal dining table is notable and suggests a desire on Washington's part to leave the center of the room unencumbered. A portable assemblage of trestles and boards, such as Washington used during the Revolutionary War, made it possible to accommodate large or small numbers of guests. When not in use, the pieces could easily be stored. At least two events of great moment occurred in this room. On April 14, 1789, during a brief ceremony, George Washington was informed of his election to the presidency by Charles Thomson, Secretary of the Congress, who had ridden from Philadelphia with this important news. Ten years later, by his own instruction, Washington's body lay here for three days before entombment. On that melancholy occasion, the household mourned the passing of its master.

SCENE ON THE HUDSON RIVER BY WILLIAM WINSTANLEY, 1793

DETAILS OF CURTAIN TREATMENTS, BASED ON A VISITOR'S DESCRIPTION OF 1798

ABOVE: PALLADIAN WINDOW ON THE NORTH WALL OF THE LARGE DINING ROOM, FLANKED BY SIDEBOARDS AND LOOKING GLASSES. A DOUBLE ROW OF SIDE CHAIRS STANDS BENEATH THE WINDOW. MATCHING FURNITURE PRESERVED A SYMMETRY IMPORTANT TO NEO-CLASSICAL TASTE. *LEFT:* EAST WALL OF THE LARGE DINING ROOM.

ABOVE: CHIMNEY WITH MARBLE MANTEL, GIVEN BY SAMUEL VAUGHAN, ON THE SOUTH WALL OF THE LARGE DINING ROOM. THE SCALE OF THIS TWO-STORY ROOM PROVIDED AMPLE SPACE FOR DINNER PARTIES AND OTHER SOCIAL FUNCTIONS. *RIGHT:* WEST WALL OF THE LARGE DINING ROOM.

THE PASSAGE

The passage, or central hall, as it was sometimes designated in early records, extends the full width of the house from the front door on the courtyard side to the piazza overlooking the river. During the warm season of the year, it was the most comfortable room in the house, and the journals of General and Mrs. Washington's visitors indicate that much of the informal social life of the home centered here. Under present-day conditions the passage serves as a point of vantage from which the visitor views the four adjoining rooms.

Between the doorways to the downstairs bedroom and the dining room hangs a key of the Bastille, a present from General Lafayette in 1790. In an accompanying letter the donor wrote:

Give me leave, my dear general, to present you with a picture of the Bastille, just as it looked a few days after I ordered its demolition, with the main key of the fortress of despotism. It is a tribute which I owe as a son to my adoptive father—as an aide-de-camp to my general—as a missionary of liberty to its patriarch.

I can truly say I had rather be at home at Mount Vernon with a friend or two about me, than to be attended at the seat of government by the officers of State and the representatives of every power in Europe.

George Washington to David Stuart, June 15, 1790

ABOVE: THE PASSAGE WHERE THE WASHINGTONS' GUESTS WERE RECEIVED. *FACING PAGE:* DETAIL OF A PLASTER LION, ONE OF A PAIR THAT STANDS ABOVE THE EAST PASSAGE DOOR.

ABOVE: PASSAGE LOOKING WEST. WASH-
INGTON'S FONDNESS FOR LANDSCAPES IS
EXPRESSED IN THE NUMEROUS ENGRAV-
INGS HUNG IN THIS AREA.

LEFT: UPPER AND LOWER PASSAGES FROM
THE LANDING

The key was transmitted by Thomas Paine, who added his own endorsement of the gift in the following words:

I feel myself happy in being the person through whom the Marquis has conveyed this early trophy of the spoils of despotism, and the first ripe fruits of American principles transplanted into Europe, to his great master and patron. . . . That the principles of America opened the Bastile is not to be doubted, and therefore the key comes to the right place.

The key was presented to the Association by Colonel John A. Washington, Jr., last private owner of Mount Vernon. It is believed to have remained continuously where it is now displayed, because it was hung there by General Washington. The case is probably contemporary. The original sketch sent by Lafayette hangs beneath the key in the location selected by Washington.

Over the double doors leading to the piazza are two plaster lions, which are authenticated by Washington descendants and identified as the "two Lyons" listed in an invoice of articles received from England in 1757. The lantern and three of the prints hanging on the walls of the lower passage are identified as original objects. The other prints are duplicates of the originals that hung here in George Washington's lifetime. The fourteen chairs arranged around the walls substitute for those listed in the inventory. They might also have provided additional seating in the rooms opening off the passage.

In 1797, Washington enhanced the passage by having it painted or grained to resemble mahogany. The technique consisted of applying a base coat of a designated color over which a glaze of the desired wood color was applied in such a way that the wood grain was simulated. The pattern for this graining was found under multiple coats of paint on the door to the blue bedroom above.

DETAIL OF THE KEY
TO THE BASTILLE

THE LITTLE PARLOR

The executors' inventory of General Washington's estate lists this room as the Little Parlor. Prior to Washington's retirement from the presidency in 1797, this small chamber had been a bedroom leaving only the more formal front parlor and the passage as the principal areas for social gatherings. To compensate for the loss of a bedroom on this floor, Washington added a third one in the garret. Julian Niemcewicz, a Polish scholar, who was a guest at Mount Vernon in June 1798, wrote a very detailed and interesting journal account of a tour of the Mansion soon after his arrival, in which he states, ". . . there is another parlor, adorned with rare engravings representing sea-scenes, and here one sees the excellent harpsichord of Miss Custis."

Music played an important part in the life of the Mount Vernon household, as in the typical Virginia home of the period. The music master rode from home to home, instructing the young, and his presence often inspired lively social gatherings at which music and dancing were the principal recreations. By his own testimony Washington could *neither sing one of the songs, nor raise a single note on any instrument*, but he loved to dance, and on one occasion during the Revolutionary War, he is reported to have danced for three hours. In the second year of his marriage George Washington ordered *1 Very good Spinit* for his stepdaughter, Patsy Custis; a few years later her brother received a violin and *a fine German flute*. At a later period the granddaughter, Nelly Custis, received instruction, advancing from the spinet to the pianoforte. In 1793, President Washington imported the handsome harpsichord from London for her use. It is, no doubt, the one to which Mr. Niemcewicz refers.

The harpsichord accompanied Nelly Custis Lewis in 1802 to her new home Woodlawn, which she and her husband, Lawrence, built on the portion of the Mount Vernon estate General Washington bequeathed to them. Many years later, when it became known that the Mount Vernon Ladies' Association would acquire and preserve Washington's home, Mrs. Lewis's daughter-in-law returned the harpsichord to Mount Vernon.

The prints over the harpsichord are duplicates of marine scenes listed in this room by General Washington's appraisers. The engraved view of the engagement between John Paul Jones's *Bonhomme Richard* and the British ship *Serapis* is identified as original to the room. Here, also, is a rare trio of

FACING PAGE: MARTHA WASHINGTON'S TEA TABLE WITH AN ARGAND LAMP. BELOW: NELLY CUSTIS'S ENGLISH HARPSICHORD IS THE PRINCIPAL PIECE OF FURNITURE IN THE LITTLE PARLOR.

mezzotints, small oval portraits of Washington, Franklin, and Lafayette, duplicates of those that hung here in Washington's lifetime.

The Windsor chairs displayed here replace those listed in the inventories. Though not original to Mount Vernon, these five chairs were made by Robert Gaw, brother of the Philadelphia chairmaker who made Windsors for George Washington. The cross-stitch chair cushions are reproductions of originals, which Mrs. Washington made for her own Windsor chairs. One of these original cushions may be seen in the museum. The ingrain carpeting is a reproduction of a type used in the Mansion by the Washingtons.

A TRIO OF RARE MEZZOTINTS OF WASHINGTON, FRANKLIN, AND LAFAYETTE
ARE SHOWN ON THE SOUTH WALL OF THE LITTLE PARLOR.

THE WEST PARLOR

Architecturally the front parlor is one of the most interesting rooms in the house; the door frames, the paneled walls, and the splendid mantel combine to make it one of the finest surviving examples of colonial Virginia interiors. In its present state, the room probably dates from the first enlargement of the house, just prior to George Washington's marriage. The dimensions of the *neat landskip*, ordered at that time through an English agent for use over a mantel, coincide with those of the painting impaneled over the mantel and probably determine its origin. The mantel design was inspired by a plate in Abraham Swan's *The British Architect . . .* , a popular eighteenth-century architectural pattern book. Prussian blue paint was introduced in 1787 when the Adamesque ceiling decoration was added to update the room. Prussian blue was an expensive pigment, having the peculiar property of deepening in color as pressure was applied to the brush, hence the irregular or striated effect, which showed up clearly in the microscopic examination of original paint chips.

In the pediment over the mantel is a carved and painted representation of the Washington family coat-of-arms. The coat-of-arms also appears in a decorative panel at the top of an original mirror, which hangs between the windows of the room. Washington's crest is cast into the iron fireback of the fireplace opening, one of four firebacks purchased in Philadelphia in 1787. Here the master's cipher, GW, replaces the mullets and bars in the

ABOVE: THE PRINCIPAL FAMILY PORTRAITS HUNG IN THE WEST PARLOR, WHERE MUCH OF THE FAMILY'S SOCIAL LIFE CENTERED. *FACING PAGE:* DETAIL OF THE WASHINGTON COAT-OF-ARMS ABOVE THE FIREPLACE. *RIGHT:* A PORTRAIT OF MARTHA WASHINGTON IS REFLECTED IN AN ORIGINAL LOOKING GLASS.

shield. Washington also used an adaptation of the coat-of-arms in his
bookplate, which appears on page 4 of this handbook. The accompanying
motto, *Exitus Acta Probat*, is freely translated, "The end proves the deed."

Before the completion of the large dining room, Washington considered this room *the best place in my House*. Here hung the more important
family portraits, thirteen by the end of his life, including the first known
portrait of the master of Mount Vernon by Charles Willson Peale. A copy of
that portrait now hangs here, together with copies of an early portrait of
Mrs. Washington and a portrait of her two children, Martha Parke and John
Parke Custis. Original portraits include the five pastels by James Sharples
(below) of General and Mrs. Washington, George Washington Lafayette,

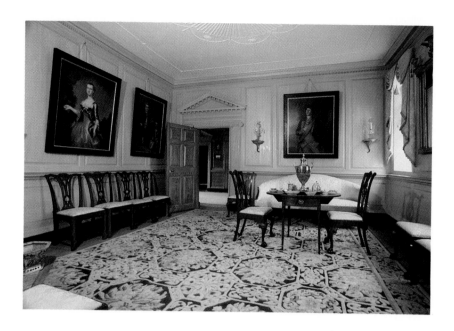

son of the Marquis, and George Washington Parke Custis and Nelly Custis, the two grandchildren raised at Mount Vernon. Other originals are the Robert Edge Pine portrait of Mrs. Washington's niece, Fanny Bassett, and the Gilbert Stuart portrait of Thomas Law, husband of Eliza Parke Custis Law. The rare emblematic engraving on satin of General Washington also hung in this room during his lifetime.

The furnishings follow the inventory listing of eleven chairs, a sofa, and tea table as the only standing furniture. The urn-shaped silver lamps and silver tray were used in Washington's presidential household. The hot water urn belonged to Martha's son, John Parke Custis, and the Chinese export porcelain tea service was hers.

55

THE SMALL DINING ROOM

The small dining room, as it has been called to distinguish it from the dining room at the north end of the house, would indeed have been too small to accommodate the numerous guests who so frequently gathered at Mount Vernon in the years after the Revolutionary War.

An air of formality is imparted to the room by the ornate mantel and decorated ceiling, executed in the autumn of 1775 by two master crafts-men, while General Washington was in command of troops outside Boston. Lund Washington, wartime manager of Mount Vernon, wrote to his em-ployer, "The dining room will I expect be finished this week now come in. It is I think, very pretty." The extraordinary vertigris green on the walls of this room was enriched by glazing, which seems to intensify the color.

WASHINGTON'S ENGLISH LIQUOR CHEST WITH ORIGINAL BOTTLES.
AN OPEN KNIFE BOX, DECANTERS, AND SILVER GRACE THE SIDEBOARD TABLE.

SMALL DINING ROOM WITH A WINE, FRUIT,
AND NUT COURSE ON THE TABLE

Washington found green to be a color *grateful to the eye* and less likely than other colors to fade.

In accordance with the evidence of the inventory compiled by General Washington's appraisers, many pictures are displayed in this room. An engraved portrait of the Washington family by Edward Savage, and engraved portraits of two famous Philadelphians, Benjamin Franklin and David Rittenhouse, are Mount Vernon memorabilia. The others, including portraits of Generals Washington, Greene, and Lafayette, are duplicates of prints listed in the room by the executors.

The mahogany table is said to be an original Mount Vernon piece, which descended in the family of Nelly Custis Lewis, Mrs. Washington's youngest granddaughter. The table setting, which consists of nuts, raisins, port and Madeira wines, is based on a description of a dinner at Mount Vernon in February 1799, left by one of the diners, Joshua Brookes, an Englishman then traveling in the United States. Such descriptions of the Washingtons' domestic life are invaluable to an authentic re-creation of the Mount Vernon environment.

The English sideboard table approximates the original piece, which disappeared during the Civil War from Arlington House, then the home of General Robert E. Lee and his wife, the great-granddaughter of Martha Washington. Of the nine original side chairs in the room (Chippendale ladder-back type), five are identical and belong to a numbered set. The looking glass, which hangs between the windows, is another original object in the room. The handsome plated wine cooler on the sideboard table was designed to keep wines cool. Decanters were supported in baskets within the cooler and surrounded by crushed ice. The large liquor chest on the floor is believed to be one imported by Colonel George Washington just after his marriage. An entry in an invoice of that period reads as

Unless some one pops in, unexpectedly, Mrs. Washington and myself will do what I believe has not been [done] within the last twenty years by us, that is to set down to dinner by ourselves.

George Washington to Tobias Lear, July 31, 1797

follows: "A neat mahogany Square Case with 16 Gall'n Bottles in ditto with ground stoppers, Brass lifting handles and brass Casters £17.17." The purchaser felt that he had been grossly overcharged and complained to his London agent, *Surely here must be as great a mistake, or as great an Imposition as ever was offered by a Tradesman.* Such complaints were common and were inherent in the tobacco economy, which existed in Virginia prior to the Revolutionary War. The planter's cash income was derived from the sale of his tobacco crop to an English merchant. The colony exported little else, and the planter's credit with the merchant was incurred to satisfy his varied needs. Under the circumstances, delays, losses, and impositions were inevitable.

CHIMNEYPIECE WITH ENGRAVING OF THE WASHINGTON FAMILY BY EDWARD SAVAGE

THE DOWNSTAIRS BEDROOM

The downstairs bedroom was a common feature of early Virginia homes. The first reference to a bedchamber on the lower floor at Mount Vernon occurs in a letter of instruction, which the young proprietor sent on to his overseer, while journeying northward from Williamsburg with his bride in the spring of 1759. This letter is now in the Mount Vernon collection and reads, in part, as follows:

You must get two of the Bedsteads put up, one in the Hall Room, and the other in the little dining Room that use to be, and have Beds made on them against we come.

The master's bedroom may have been on the first floor until the addition to the south end of the house was completed in 1775; the surviving domestic records offer no further information on the subject.

Even after the house was enlarged, there would have been a continuing need for a sleeping chamber on the first floor. The post–Revolutionary War

family numbered eight persons: General and Mrs. Washington; the two Custis grandchildren; the General's nephew, George Augustine Washington, and his wife; and the two secretaries, Colonel Humphreys and Tobias Lear. This family-in-residence would have fully occupied the rooms on the second floor. The numerous overnight guests so frequently noted in General Washington's diary must have taxed the facilities of the house.

Room designations in the later years of General and Mrs. Washington's occupancy are more specifically recorded in several references. They reveal that there were, at one time, two bedrooms on the first floor, but that one was refurnished as a parlor in 1797, when the family returned from Philadelphia, bringing many pieces of furniture with them. This room continued to serve as a bedroom until the end of General Washington's life. The large oil painting depicts the 1759 battle of Minden in which Lafayette's father was killed. It was a gift to Washington in 1787 from Samuel Vaughan and originally hung in the large dining room before being moved here by Washington to make room for the moonlight painting that now hangs over the Vaughan mantel. The upholstered chair is an original piece and was known in the family as Martha Washington's sewing chair.

THE UPPER CHAMBERS

There are five bedchambers on the second floor of the Mansion, in addition to the master's sleeping quarters over the study. The first room at the head of the central stairway was called the blue bedroom, a name derived apparently from the color of its woodwork. A section of the original graining may be seen on the door of this room. Adjoining was the Lafayette room, so called after its most distinguished occupant, who slept here in 1784 on the occasion of his last visit with General Washington. The small room to the right of the garret stairway is the only one on the floor without a fireplace. Originally this space and the adjoining stairway had formed a storage room, which Washington partitioned when he added the garret in 1758.

On the south side of the hall is the yellow room, where an English chest of drawers, original to the room, may be seen. It was purchased by Washington in 1757 and is equipped with a writing slide and compartmented top drawer, which served as a dressing table. The Nelly Custis

For in truth it may be compared to a well resorted tavern, as scarcely any strangers who are going from north to south, or from south to north, do not spend a day or two at it.

George Washington to Mary Washington, February 15, 1787

FACING PAGE: THE BLUE BEDROOM. *ABOVE:* NORTHEAST CHAMBER WHERE LAFAYETTE STAYED IN 1784.

DETAIL OF MARTHA WASHINGTON'S
CHINESE DRESSING GLASS AND TEA SERVICE
IN THE LAFAYETTE BEDROOM

room bears the name of Mrs. Washington's youngest granddaughter, who was a member of the Mount Vernon household from childhood. On General Washington's last birthday, February 22, 1799, she married his nephew, Lawrence Lewis, who had come to Mount Vernon in 1797 at his uncle's request to assist him in a secretarial and social capacity. In this room is the crib, which was used by their first child.

The walls of some of these rooms are known to have been papered originally, but the original designs have not survived. By the 1780s plain wallpaper with applied border was in fashion and Washington adopted that decoration for Nelly Custis's room and the yellow bedroom. The second floor is an interesting study of the variety of shades of Prussian blue that could be attained by adjusting paint formulas.

The Washington servants were kept busy preparing the rooms for the numerous guests who found their way to Washington's door. Mrs. Washington kept low post beds in the garret, which were brought down and set up in the rooms to accommodate the overflow. With the travelers' trunks and boxes in place, the bedrooms would have presented a busy scene.

When the Washingtons returned to Mount Vernon from Philadelphia in 1797 they brought with them "one Tin Shower bath." No other description exists, but an inventory of the contents of the Mansion prepared for Mrs. Washington's estate seems to indicate that it was installed under the stairs leading to the third floor. It is unfortunate that such a unique convenience has not survived.

INSIDE THE TRUNK, A FACSIMILE OF A LETTER IN WHICH ELIZA PARKE CUSTIS DESCRIBED HER GRANDMOTHER'S WARTIME TRAVELS

HALL BEDROOM, SHOWING WINDSOR CHAIRS

There are fewer noteworthy objects in these chambers than in the rooms on the lower floor, but a number deserve notice. On the third floor is the trunk that accompanied Mrs. Washington on her journeys to and from the winter quarters of the American army during the Revolutionary War. Affixed to the lid of the trunk is a letter in which Mrs. Washington's eldest granddaughter describes for her grandchildren how she watched her grandmother pack in the fall, "sadly distressed at her going away," and in the spring, the letter relates, "Oh how joyfully did I look on to see her cloaths taken out, & the many gifts she always brought for her grandchildren!"

There are seven rooms on the third floor of the Mansion, three of which are furnished as bedrooms to conform with the inventory compiled after General Washington's death. These provided sleeping quarters for the visitors who could not be accommodated on the floor below. On the death

At twelve I had the honor of being lighted up to my bed room by the General himself.
Diary of Robert Hunter, Jr., 1785

South corner of the Nelly Custis bedroom.

LEFT AND ABOVE: THE YELLOW BEDROOM AND DE-TAIL OF THE CHEST OF DRAWERS, SHOWING THE TOP DRAWER, WHICH IS COMPARTMENTED FOR COS-METICS AND OTHER ARTICLES

BELOW: THE NELLY CUSTIS BEDROOM, SHOWING CRIB GIVEN TO NELLY CUSTIS BY MARTHA WASH-INGTON.

GARRET CHAMBER USED BY MARTHA WASHINGTON AFTER WASHINGTON'S DEATH IN 1799

of her husband, Martha Washington closed the second floor bedroom they had shared for nearly a quarter century. Such tributes to the deceased were customary in the eighteenth century, but rarely for indefinite periods. Mrs. Washington moved to the bedroom in the garret that Washington furnished in 1797 when he converted a first floor bedroom into a parlor. The addition of a Franklin fireplace provided the necessary heat source for Mrs. Washington's bedroom. She continued to manage her household, and numerous guests wrote of visiting with her at this period. Her garret room was a cheerful place, and her grandson's presence across the hall was comforting. After two and one-half years of widowhood, Martha Washington died in this room on May 22, 1802.

The remaining rooms in this area of the house are identified as lumber rooms, an eighteenth-century term for storerooms. During the fall and winter months when the visitation is relatively light, the third floor is open to the public.

ABOVE: FIREPLACE IN A GARRET BEDROOM
BELOW: OVAL WINDOW IN A SMALL CLOSET WHERE
GLASS AND CHINA WERE KEPT

69

GENERAL AND MRS. WASHINGTON'S
BEDCHAMBER

This room and the adjoining closets constitute the second floor of the
south addition to the Mansion. A narrow stairway from the floor below
afforded the master and mistress a measure of privacy in a house constantly filled with guests.

In this room and on this bed, George Washington answered the final
summons on December 14, 1799. Mrs. Washington bequeathed the bed,
which she had had made in Philadelphia about 1794, to her grandson,
George Washington Parke Custis. Her bequest reveals that the bed hangings were made of white dimity, a ribbed cotton fabric popular in the
eighteenth century. The present dimity bed and window hangings were

Martha Washington's French desk

THE BEDSTEAD ON WHICH GEORGE WASHINGTON DIED

reproduced from an original fragment in the Mount Vernon collections. After Mrs. Washington's death, the bed was carefully preserved at Arlington House by her grandson. In 1908, through the generosity of his descendants, it was returned to its accustomed place. The unusual width of the bed and the height of the posts cause it to appear short; it is six and one-half feet long.

Mrs. Washington used this room in much the same way her husband used his study below. Management of a large and busy household took time, and she did not always have a housekeeper to assist. Here she read daily from the New Testament, and, though a reluctant correspondent, did her duty in this matter as in all others. Her French desk is probably the one listed in a memorandum of furniture purchased in 1791 from the Comte de Moustier, first French minister to this country. On top of the desk is her leather key basket, a most important accessory in her daily inspection of the rooms and buildings under her direct supervision.

The portraits are of her four grandchildren, Eliza Parke Custis, Martha Parke Custis, Eleanor (Nelly) Parke Custis, and George Washington Parke Custis. Martha and Nelly's portraits are originals by Robert Edge Pine and the others, copies of Pine's 1785 studies. The six round engravings, scenes from contemporary literature, were Mrs. Washington's selections. Mrs. Washington's knee-hole dressing table, one of the few Virginia-made pieces

When the summons comes I shall endeavor to obey it with a good grace.
George Washington to Burges Ball, September 22, 1799

in the Mansion, and the Chinese lacquered dressing glass were returned by her descendants. The easy chair is a copy of the original.

The closet on the left was used for the best linens and the one on the right for dressing and storage. The plain whitewashed walls were Mrs. Washington's preference, and the pale Prussian blue paint is a restoration of the original color. Natural pine floors, here and throughout the house, were characteristic of the eighteenth century.

A detailed account of General Washington's illness and death is contained in a letter from his secretary, Tobias Lear, which is in the Mount Vernon collection. A briefer contemporary account, from a letter published by a Boston paper a few days after the event, reads in part as follows:

The General, a little time before his death, had begun several improvements on his farm. Attending to some of these he probably caught his death. He had in contemplation a gravel walk on the banks of the Potomac; between the walk and the river there was to be a fish-pond. Some trees were to be cut down, and others preserved. On Friday, the day before he died, he spent some time by the side of the river, marking the former. There came a fall of snow, which did not deter him from his pursuit, but he continued till his neck and hair were quite covered with snow. He spent the evening with Mrs. Washington, reading the newspaper, which came by the mail of that evening; went to bed as usual about nine o'clock, waked up in the night, found himself extremely unwell, but would not allow Mrs. Washington to get up, or the servants to be waked. In the morning, finding himself very ill, Dr. Craik of Alexandria was sent for. Soon after his arrival, the two consulting physicians were called in, but all would not avail. On Saturday evening he died.

MARTHA PARKE CUSTIS
BY ROBERT EDGE PINE

WASHINGTON'S FRENCH MANTEL CLOCK

73

THE STUDY

The study was an important feature of the enlarged Mansion. The addition at the south end, of which it forms a part, had been enclosed under the master's direction before he departed to attend the second Continental Congress in May 1775. The interior was finished under the direction of his manager, Lund Washington, before the end of the year; the library bookpress was not installed until 1786. At that time, all the pine woodwork in the study was painted to simulate a finer wood. Known as graining, it appears elsewhere in the Mansion.

The addition to the north end of the house corresponds outwardly with that at the south end. The former was planned to provide a single large room, adequate to the demands upon the hospitality of the house. The

latter provided quarters to which the master could retire from ever-present family and company to carry on his essential activities. This room was the headquarters from which he directed the management of his estate. Here he received the reports of his overseers, made daily entries in his diary, and posted his accounts.

In this room, during the critical years following the close of the war, General Washington penned the letters that gave decisive impetus to the movement toward the establishment of a federal government. Here, at this period, was what a contemporary writer called "the focus of political intelligence for the new world." No private chamber in the land has more fruitful associations with his life at Mount Vernon. It was to this room that he came immediately upon arising, often before sunrise, and prepared himself for the day's activities. His dressing table, a French piece purchased during the presidency, stands between the windows.

ABOVE: FINE BINDINGS OF ORIGINAL VOLUMES
FROM GEORGE WASHINGTON'S LIBRARY. *RIGHT:*
WATERMARK FROM GEORGE WASHINGTON'S
WRITING PAPER. *BELOW:* GEORGE WASHING-
TON'S COPY OF ROBERT BURNS'S *POEMS* . . .
NEW YORK, 1788, WITH HIS CHARACTERISTIC
SIGNATURE ON THE TITLE PAGE.

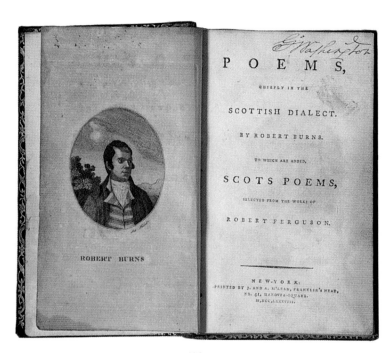

WASHINGTON'S PRESIDENTIAL DESK CHAIR AND A TAMBOUR SECRETARY MADE FOR MOUNT VERNON

FAN CHAIR SIMILAR TO ONE OWNED BY WASHINGTON

PLASTER PROFILE OF
GEORGE WASHINGTON
BY JOSEPH WRIGHT

PORTRAIT OF LAWRENCE WASHINGTON

At the close of his presidency, Washington disposed of the desk that he had used in Philadelphia, and there purchased the tambour secretary made for this room by John Aitken. The accompanying chair is also original. Desk and chair were bequeathed to Dr. James Craik, who had been closely associated with Washington since 1754 and attended him in his fatal illness. The desk remained in the possession of descendants until 1905, when it was acquired by the Association and returned to its original position. The chair was presented by the family of Dr. Craik's granddaughter to Andrew Jackson, in token of admiration, and acquired, also in 1905, from General Jackson's heirs.

The terrestrial globe, which stands near the bookpress, is an original piece, which remained at Mount Vernon and was presented to the Association by the last private owner, Colonel John A. Washington, Jr. It was made in London on General Washington's order, and reached him in New York during the first year of his presidency.

The executors' inventory lists busts of General Washington and John Paul Jones in this room. The former was the bust by Houdon, which is now displayed in the musuem. In its place here is a copy by Clark Mills. The bust of Jones, also by Houdon, was lost by fire in Alexandria many years ago; its place is filled by a copy of another bust portrait of Jones by the

same sculptor. The bas relief profile of General Washington was done by Joseph Wright in 1785 in the classical pose that became popular for national heroes after the Revolutionary War.

The whip stock on the table, the large ducking gun in the corner, and the gold-headed walking staff by the desk are authenticated as Washington memorabilia. Over the dressing table hangs a portrait of Lawrence Washington, elder half brother, which was listed in this room by General Washington's appraisers. The small walnut table is said to be the one at which the Washingtons ate their wedding breakfast at the home of the bride, where they were married on January 6, 1759. The iron chest belonged to Mrs. Washington's first husband, Daniel Parke Custis, and was used later by George Washington to secure valuable objects and papers. The barometer is said to be an original object, a reminder of General Washington's interest in all that affected his farming activities. Through the years, the state of the weather was regularly noted in his daily diary entries.

The fan chair, an eighteenth-century piece, replaced the original, which was sold out of the family in 1802. Washington bought one in 1787, shortly after its innovation by John Cram of Philadelphia for Charles Willson Peale. The fan apparatus could be adapted to any Windsor chair and was activated by operating the pedals.

The inventory of George Washington's library prepared after his death listed 884 bound volumes, numerous pamphlets, and a comprehensive collection of maps. The titles reflect Washington's wide-ranging interests and the many roles he played in his life: soldier, statesman, farmer, businessman, and gentleman. The library was particularly strong in works of

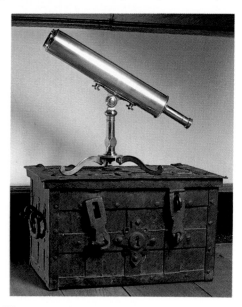

WASHINGTON'S BRASS TELESCOPE AND IRON CHEST

history, politics, law, agriculture, military strategy, literature, and geography. There is evidence of Washington's practical bent in his first order to his English agent after his marriage. Among several books requested was Batty Langley's *New Principles of Gardening*, a popular guide published in London in 1728. Langley was an early advocate of the English naturalistic style of landscape design, and Washington was profoundly influenced by Langley's theories and vocabulary in laying out his own estate. Along with his order for Langley, Washington requested a book *call'd a New System of Agriculture, or a Speedy Way to grow Rich*. Later, in Philadelphia a few days before accepting command of the Continental Army, he noted an expenditure in his pocket memorandum book, *By 5 books—Military 1.12.0*. As the war drew to an end, his account books reveal that he was seeking out works of literature and travel guides in anticipation of the leisure that would come with peace. Many of the books in the library were gifts to Washington from friends and admirers and, as his prominence grew, many American publications were dedicated to him. Washington also bought books for the edification of the many young people in his household, including Mrs. Washington's children and grandchildren and the many nephews and nieces who spent time at Mount Vernon.

Washington's library was bequeathed to his nephew and principal heir, Bushrod Washington, a Justice of the Supreme Court of the United States, together with *all the Papers in my possession, which relate to my Civel and Military Administration of the affairs of this Country [and] such of my private Papers as are worth preserving*. Judge Washington, by bequest, divided this priceless collection of books and papers between two of his nephews, George C. and John Augustine Washington. The civil and military papers were sold to the federal government prior to 1850 and are now in the manuscript division of the Library of Congress. In 1848, the Boston Atheneum acquired more than 350 of General Washington's books from a dealer who had purchased them. The remainder of the library has been widely dispersed through the years. By gift and purchase, the Association has acquired more than 75 of these scattered volumes. More than 300 of the remaining titles listed in the executors' inventory are represented in the collection by duplicates of the same imprints.

General Washington's books were customarily identified by his signature on the title page. Some also contain his bookplate, an adaptation of the family coat-of-arms. A reproduction of his bookplate appears on page 4 of this handbook. Books exhibiting the bookplate and typical signature are displayed in the musuem.

THE PANTRY

The pantry is identified in the appraisers' inventory as "the Closet under Franks direction." Frank Lee, a slave, and the son of Washington's valet, William Lee, was the butler, or steward, and occupied quarters in the basement, where there was also a white servants' dining room. The family tableware in daily use was kept here. The finer chinaware was stored in an upstairs closet. A reference in Mrs. Washington's will to "the blew and white China in common use" identifies the china that would have been "under Franks direction" in this pantry. Of this original blue-and-white Canton china, only a few scattered pieces have survived; several of these are displayed in the museum. A similar service was owned by Mrs. Samuel Powel of Philadelphia, a close friend of the Washingtons. This china has been carefully cherished and more than one hundred surviving pieces are now displayed here, the gift of a member of the Powel family.

Food was prepared in the kitchen and brought into the house by way of the adjoining colonnade. Across the ceilings of the back hall and pantry may still be seen evidence of the wiring for the house bell system, which terminated in a row of bells on the south end of the Mansion. In this way the servants could be summoned if needed in the dining room or on the piazza, where the family often took tea on pleasant days.

The closet in the back of the pantry was used by General Washington for his personal possessions. His use of inexpensive black paint in a "non-public" area was a typical economy of the great man. On the floor of the closet is an:

exact model of the Bastile, made from the very materials of this once celebrated fortress. . . . The model . . . is admitted to be the only one of the kind in existence, except those made by order by the National Assembly for each of the Departments of France. . . .

of which there were then eighty-three. The model was a gift to President Washington from a Mr. Slade, an English admirer of Washington, and was sent to Philadelphia by Sam Bayard, whose letter of July 28, 1795, is quoted above. During Washington's lifetime, the model stood on the piazza, a plaything for the children of the household.

I wish you to have all the china looked over, the closet cleansed and the glasses all washed and everything in the closet as clean as can be.
    Martha Washington to her niece, July 1, 1792

82

THE KITCHEN

By the terms of George Washington's will, the *household & Kitchen furniture of every sort & kind, with the liquors and groceries* were bequeathed to Mrs. Washington, *to be used and disposed of as she may think proper.* Few of these original kitchen furniture and utensils survive, as they continued in use and were valued less than the finer furnishings of the Mansion. The crane in the kitchen fireplace is believed to be an original, as are some of the six pewter plates with hot-water compartments, a trivet, an iron-stand, a marble mortar and a bell metal skillet. The other utensils shown in the kitchen are from the period and include a number from the home of one of Mrs. Washington's granddaughters.

George Washington once described his life style to a friend: *My manner of living is plain, and I do not mean to be put out of it. A glass of wine and a bit of mutton are always ready, and such as will be content to partake of them are always welcome. Those who expect more will be disappointed.* Yet there is ample evidence that the fare served at Mount Vernon was more elegant and sophisticated than Washington suggested. The generosity of his table is indicated by one guest who commented, "The dinner was very good, a small roasted pigg, boiled leg of lamb, roasted fowls, beef, peas, lettuce, cucumbers, artichokes, etc., puddings, tarts, etc. etc. We were desired to call for what drinks we chose."

The choice of drink at dinner included a variety of wines, beer, and cider. General Washington's preference was for a fine Madeira wine. After dinner, he remained at the table for an hour or longer, conversing with guests as toasts were offered to absent friends and favored causes.

INTERIOR OF THE LARDER

MARBLE MORTAR AND BELL METAL SKILLET

LEFT: MARTHA WASHINGTON'S
    PRESERVING POT

It was a rare occasion when there were no guests at a meal. Several months after retiring from the presidency, Washington noted in a letter that he and Mrs. Washington were sitting down to dinner alone, something they had not done *for twenty years.* In another letter, he regretfully commented on meals which always seemed to bring new guests: *I rarely miss seeing strange faces, come as they say out of respect for me. Pray, would not the word curiosity answer as well? And how different this from having a few social friends at a cheerful board...*

After the Revolutionary War, the normal household staff included two cooks and two waiters, under the direction of a steward. This staff worked constantly and was ready at a moment's notice to serve an additional guest at a meal or prepare a plate for a late-arriving visitor. Breakfast was at seven. According to one visitor it was served "in the usual Virginia style," consisting of tea, coffee, cold meat and boiled meat. Yet many sources record Washington's usual breakfast as "three small mush cakes...swimming in butter and honey," accompanied by "three cups of tea without cream." Dinner, the main meal of the day, was served at three. Tea was served about six, and supper—a light meal—was not served at all according to one visitor, but was offered at nine according to another.

The hospitality of Mount Vernon was not restricted to those who warranted a seat at the master's table. General Washington's generosity with his larder and his purse benefitted those less fortunate. In 1775 he wrote from his military headquarters in Cambridge to his manager, Lund Washington: *Let the Hospitality of the House, with respect to the poor, be kept up; Let no one go hungry away. If any of these kind of People should be in want of Corn, supply their necessities...and I have no objection to your giving my Money in Charity, to the Amount of forty or fifty Pounds a Year...*

Opposite the large kitchen are two rooms. The scullery, on the right, provided additional space for food preparation and for dishwashing. The Chinese porcelain dishes with their distinctive blue and white pattern are from the period and were "the dishes in common use" according to Mrs. Washington. The stairway leads to two rooms upstairs used for storing kitchen utensils and as an apartment for the housekeeper. At the time of George Washington's death, the housekeeper was a white servant named Mrs. Forbes, who came to Mount Vernon after working in the same capacity for the governor of Virginia.

The second room, a larder, was cooler than the rest of the kitchen as a result of being partially underground. With the door closed to keep out the heat from the fireplace, perishables would keep here for a day or two. Over the years George Washington tried with varying degrees of success to fill an icehouse with enough ice cut from the river each winter to last through the hot Virginia summer.

THE NORTH LANE

The north lane leads northward from the circle in front of the Mansion, and is a service lane, lined with outbuildings. These attractive buildings, most covered in white clapboard and roofed with red-painted wood shingles, provided work spaces for some of the activities of the Mount Vernon plantation and housing for many of its slaves.

The first building on the lane was listed by an assessor in 1799 as the "Gardiners House." Yet when it was constructed, nearly a quarter of a century before, it was intended as an infirmary where slaves could be warmly housed and cared for during illnesses. It was put to other uses as well, depending on the rate at which new buildings were completed and the family size of various employees. At one period, it was designated the "Shoemaker and Taylors apartment." The shoemaker and tailor were full-time positions at Mount Vernon, sometimes filled by slave craftsmen, sometimes by hired tradesmen. In meeting the needs for Mount Vernon, the shoemaker in one year is credited with making 217 pairs of shoes while mending another 199 pairs.

The salt house, located just behind the gardener's house, was intended for storage with its windowless design. It was filled with many of the supplies needed for Washington's fishing operation, the most important of which was salt. Washington developed an extensive and profitable fishing enterprise, harvesting huge quantities of shad, herring and sturgeon that migrated up the Potomac every spring. After the fish were thoroughly

A SALT BARREL IN THE SALT HOUSE.

SHEEP ARE SHEARED BY HAND, AS THEY WERE IN WASHINGTON'S TIME,
TO PROVIDE WOOL FOR SPINNING.

cleaned and prepared, they were packed in barrels with salt. The salt kept the fish from spoiling, allowing it to be stored for consumption the following winter or shipped to markets overseas.

Salt was the primary means of preserving meat, because it prevented the growth of bacteria and helped dry the meat by drawing out moisture. Washington constantly sought a reliable supply of high-quality salt, importing it from as far away as Portugal.

The salt house also held other supplies, including the heavy nets used at the fishery, some as long as one hundred yards, and oars and repair materials for the boats. Inventories indicate that scrap iron used by the blacksmith was also stored here, and probably spare tools as well.

The spinning house was the most important structure on the north lane. At Mount Vernon ten or more slaves were constantly employed spinning and knitting. A number of them were unable to work at more strenuous jobs, including "Lame Peter," Winny, who was described as "old & almost blind" and women recovering from childbirth. The spinning equipment and fibers were stored in the spinning house, while the work of spinning took place in the homes of the slaves or in outside work yards. The fibers used were all produced on the estate and included large

ABOVE: THE OVERSEER'S QUARTERS

FACING PAGE: GEORGE WASHINGTON'S DRAWING OF THE PLAN FOR THE GREENHOUSE
AND SLAVE QUARTERS, C. 1785

quantities of linen grown from flax, wool sheared from sheep, and smaller quantities of cotton. The reels, spinning wheels, carders and other tools displayed in the spinning room are representative of the equipment originally stored there. Some of them were collected in the Mount Vernon neighborhood.

Weaving was usually conducted by an itinerant tradesman, who traveled with his loom and would work for weeks converting the homespun threads and yarns into cloth. A surviving account book documents the work of Thomas Davis, a hired weaver, between 1767 and 1771. In 1768 Davis is recorded as having produced 815 yards of linen, 165 yards of woolen cloth, 144 yards of linsey-woolsey (a combination of wool and linen), and 40 yards of cotton. This quantity of cloth was used almost entirely in clothing the slave population of Mount Vernon.

The loomed fabric was turned over to slave seamstresses, who produced the finished clothing. Work pants, shirts, jackets and stockings were made in both wool and linsey-woolsey for winter use, and in lighter linen for summer wear. Slaves were usually issued two sets of clothing each year.

The overseer's quarters was a residence often used by one of the overseers of Mount Vernon's slaves. George Washington usually placed an overseer at each of Mount Vernon's five farms to supervise the slave crews who lived and worked at that farm. At times these positions were held by slaves, who in turn reported directly to Washington or to an overall farm manager.

Washington set guidelines for his overseers, and counseled them in their management of the slaves. He discouraged physical punishment, viewing it primarily as a penalty for wrongdoing, and then only after an inquiry established a slave's guilt. To motivate the slaves to work, he advised his overseers to give *advice and admonition,* accompanied by such close supervision that slaves were kept at their tasks. In addition, slaves received improved food rations and cash bonuses while engaged in the most taxing jobs and occasionally had the opportunity of advancing to more desirable positions.

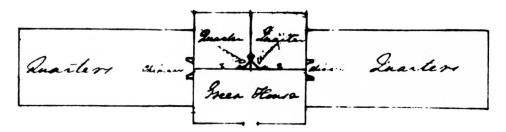

The slave quarters along the north lane were constructed in 1792, completing a final part of Washington's plan for the grounds around Mount Vernon. The quarters are located in brick wings of a greenhouse that was completed about seven years earlier. The greenhouse and slave quarters burned in 1835, but were reconstructed in 1951 on the original foundation, following Washington's plans for the building and guided by an early 19th-century sketch made as part of an insurance policy on the building.

With the completion of the greenhouse slave quarters, Washington demolished an older two-story *house for families* in the area. The new brick slave quarters provided housing for many of the ninety slaves at the Mansion House Farm. While no details are known about their living arrangements, Washington instructed the slave bricklayers and carpenters to install *sleeping births* in the quarters, which were probably bunk-style beds similar to those used by soldiers in the Revolution. Slaves also lived in some of the other outbuildings and in nearby cabins *of their own building.*

Slaves at the Mansion House Farm were predominately skilled workers, who provided the labor and talents to construct buildings and make tools, run special enterprises at Mount Vernon, care for and train horses and mules, tend the gardens, prepare food, and serve in the Mansion. Among the men, their skills included blacksmiths, carpenters, gardeners, shoemakers, painters, brickmakers, and plasters. There were also millers and coopers, who lived and worked at the gristmill, about three miles from the Mansion, boatmen who operated Washington's river ferry and conducted his fishing operation, and overseers who directed the work of other slaves. Others worked as servants in the Mansion, as coachmen and as cooks. Women at the Mansion House Farm were spinners, seamstresses, dairy maids, cooks, scullery maids and laundresses.

The work week at Mount Vernon, for slaves and hired workers, was Monday through Saturday, beginning at sunrise and not ending until sunset. As demanding as this schedule was, the slaves developed a strong community with active personal lives. Washington's slave census of 1799 reveals that two-thirds of the adults above the age of twenty were married and that three-quarters of the children under the age of fourteen had both a mother and father living on the estate. Married couples, however, did not always live together. Marriage might bring together slaves living on different farms at Mount Vernon, and work assignments would require the mother and children to live at one farm while the father lived and worked at another. The census also reveals that several of the slaves were married to slaves from other plantations and one woman was married to a free black living in Georgetown.

INTERIOR OF SLAVE QUARTERS IN THE GREENHOUSE COMPLEX

In addition to family, Mount Vernon slaves were able to travel in the immediate area, pursue limited business opportunities and spend time socializing. Slaves gardens were common, and were almost a necessity to supplement the tedious ration of cornmeal, dried fish and meat that Washington provided. But slaves also sold vegetables, eggs, chickens, handmade brooms, and baskets at market in Alexandria, as well as to the Washingtons. Evidence of a surprisingly open and strong economy is indicated by an entry in Washington's account books in 1798, recording the sale of 35-1/2 gallons of whiskey to Nat, a slave blacksmith, possibly for resale. Leisure time activities included music and singing, an occasional trip to Alexandria for events such as a horse race, and very likely informal religious services that blossomed into one of the first black churches in the area in the early 19th century.

93

THE SOUTH LANE

The lane south from the Mansion circle leads to a series of outbuildings and the stable. At the top of the lane, across from the kitchen, is a combined storehouse and clerk's quarters. The storehouse provided secure storage for hundreds of items such as tools and nails used by carpenters, leather and thread for the cobbler, powder and shot for the huntsmen, and blankets and clothes worn by the slaves. Items were inventoried as they were purchased and then carefully issued to slave craftsmen as needed for work at Mount Vernon.

LEFT: INTERIOR OF THE STOREHOUSE WITH WASHINGTON'S PACKING CASE AND A TERRA-COTTA SOAP JAR IN THE FOREGROUND.

BELOW: EXTERIOR OF THE CIRCLE STOREHOUSE.

The clerk's quarters are in the same building, and provided a residence and office for Washington's secretary. After the presidency, this position was filled by Albin Rawlings, who assisted Washington with his correspondence and served as a business agent, helping to run enterprises such as the gristmill. The cellar of the building was used for paint storage, housing the expensive pigments that were painstakingly ground by hand and mixed with linseed oil to create house paint.

The smokehouse seems scarcely adequate in size to have smoked and dried the quantities of pork, bacon and ham that were consumed at Mount Vernon. In January 1776, General Washington received a glowing letter from his farm manager, Lund Washington, reporting that 132 hogs had been slaughtered: "When I put it up I expected Mrs. Washington would live at home, if you did not, and was I to judge the future from the past consumption, there would have been a use for it, —for I believe Mrs. Washington's charitable disposition increases in the same proportion with her meat house."

CLERK'S QUARTERS

WASHHOUSE ON THE SOUTH LANE.

The washhouse was staffed by two slave women who had a heavy workload, keeping clothing and linens washed and ironed. Their task increased with the arrival of guests, as one visitor noted that the slaves "took care of me, of my linen, of my clothes," treating him "not as a stranger but as a member of the family." With the confusing mix of family and guests, the washhouse slaves were known to embroider the initials of the owner on articles of clothing to avoid mix-ups as the laundry was sorted. Clothes were washed with lye soap in hot water, rinsed and then hung to dry in the laundry yard behind. After being ironed and folded, the clean clothes and linens were returned to their owners.

THE LAUNDRY YARD BEHIND THE OUTBUILDINGS ON THE SOUTH LANE.

...From the clangor of arms and the bustle of a camp, freed from the cares of public employment, and the responsibility of office, I am now enjoying domestic ease under the shadow of my own Vine, and my own Fig tree; and in a small Villa, with the implements of Husbandry, and Lambkins around me, I expect to glide gently down the stream of life...
Washington to Marchioness de Lafayette, April 4, 1784

THE STABLE

The brick stable at the foot of the south lane was built in 1782, replacing a frame stable on the same site that had been destroyed by fire the previous year. The stable was reserved for the use of the family's coach and saddle horses, and the horses of the hundreds of people who visited the General each year. These extra animals were a financial burden and greatly increased the workload of the slaves at the stable. A young Englishman who visited Mount Vernon in 1785 described some of the horses kept in the stable:

"After breakfast I went with Shaw to see his [General Washington's] famous racehorse, 'Magnolia,' a most beautiful creature...I afterwards went into his stables, where among an amazing number of horses I saw old 'Nelson,' now twenty-two years of age, that carried the General almost always during the war. 'Blueskin,' another fine old horse next to him, now and then had that honor. They have heard the roaring of many a cannon in their time. 'Blueskin' was not the favorite, on account of his not standing fire so well as venerable old 'Nelson.' The General makes no manner of use of them now; he keeps them in a nice stable, where they feed away at their ease for their past services."

Magnolia was an Arabian stallion that George Washington raced in Alexandria. Nelson was the valued gift of General Thomas Nelson of Yorktown.

General Washington's contemporaries regarded him as an outstanding horseman. Thomas Jefferson considered Washington the "best horseman of his age." The Marquis de Chastellux, who visited him at his army headquarters, provided more detail:

"The weather being fair, on the 26th, I got on horseback, after breakfasting with the General. He was so attentive as to give me the horse he rode on, the day of my arrival, which I had greatly commended; I found him as good as he is handsome; but above all, perfectly well broke, and well trained having a good mouth, easy in hand, and stopping short in a gallop without bearing the bit. I mention these minute particulars, because it is the General himself who breaks all his own horses; and he is a very excellent and bold horseman, leaping the highest fences, and going extremely quick, without standing upon his stirrups, bearing on the bridel, or letting his horse run wild."

When at home the master of Mount Vernon delighted in fox hunting. He maintained a pack of foxhounds and hunted frequently with his neighbors; in 1768 alone, he went fox hunting on fifty separate occasions. During the hunting season the hounds accompanied him two or three times a week on his daily tour of the farms. Although they frequently raised a fox, Washington often noted in his diary, *catch'd nothing*. One of these unsuccessful forays occurred after he had *run a fox from 11 Oclock until near 3 Oclock*.

THE STABLE, BUILT IN 1782 ALONG THE SOUTH LANE.
THE STABLE SHELTERED THE WASHINGTONS' SADDLE
HORSES AND THE FAMILY COACH.

The coach compartment of the stable housed the family coach. From 1768, when he ordered an English chariot *in newest taste, handsome, genteel and light*, until the end of his life, General Washington maintained a succession of fashionable carriages. None has survived. The coach in use at the time of his death was purchased by Mrs. Washington's grandson; a later owner cut it in pieces to distribute as souvenirs of the original owner. The coach compartment now contains one of the few surviving coaches from the period. It belonged to Mayor Samuel Powel of Philadelphia and his wife, who were friends of the Washingtons during the presidency and earlier. It is believed to be nearly identical to the Washingtons' coach, and was built by the same Philadelphia coachmaker.

The two-wheeled riding chair in the coach house is a unique survival of one of the most common conveyances in colonial Virginia. This simple

vehicle is authenticated by family tradition as having belonged to George Washington's friend and patron, Thomas, Lord Fairfax. Local tax records indicate that Washington owned both a light carriage and a riding chair before the Revolutionary War, but he gave up the riding chair after the war in favor of a light chaise.

Behind the stable is a shed-like extension where mules were tethered. Among George Washington's accomplishments was the introduction of mules to the United States. Beginning with a male jackass named Royal Gift, a present from the King of Spain, Washington carried out an intensive breeding program under the direction of a slave named Peter Hardman. The results are evident in two inventories of Mount Vernon livestock: one taken in 1785 listed 130 working horses and no mules, the second, taken in 1799, recorded 25 horses and 58 mules.

POWEL COACH

LORD FAIRFAX'S RIDING CHAIR

MULE SHED BEHIND THE STABLE

THE TOMB

"Within this Enclosure Rest the remains of Gen.¹ George Washington."
This is the brief legend inscribed on a stone tablet over the entrance to the
vault. Behind the iron gate are two marble sarcophagi, one inscribed
"Washington," the other "Martha, Consort of Washington."

General Washington's will directed the building of the present vault in
the following words:

> *The family Vault at Mount Vernon requiring repairs, and being im-
> properly situated besides, I desire that a new one of Brick, and upon a larger
> Scale, may be built at the foot of what is commonly called the Vineyard
> Inclosure,—on the ground which is marked out.—In which my remains, with
> those of my deceased relatives (now in the old Vault) and such others of my
> family as may chuse to be entombed there, may be deposited.*

The Reverend Thomas Davis, Rector of Christ Church in Alexandria,
read the Episcopal burial service at the time of Washington's entombment

TOMB OF WASHINGTON.

DETAIL OF WASHINGTON'S
MARBLE SARCOPHAGUS

A CONTEMPORARY VIEW OF THE
OLD BURIAL VAULT AT MOUNT
VERNON AS IT APPEARED BEFORE
THE NEW TOMB WAS BUILT IN 1831

and delivered a brief extemporaneous eulogy. His Masonic brethren performed their graveside ritual. George Washington attended church regularly throughout his life, while at home and during his long absences. Until Pohick Church fell into disuse after the Revolutionary War, he attended there most frequently, although he purchased a pew at Christ Church, Alexandria, in 1773. Before the Revolution brought about the dissolution of the established church in Virginia, he conformed to its usages and rendered faithful service as a lay official. He continued to support its clergy during the difficult period of transition from which emerged the present Protestant Episcopal Church.

General Washington's career and writings manifest a deep and abiding faith; religion was a guiding influence in his life, both public and private. This influence is nowhere more happily displayed than in the closing sen-

And it is my express desire that my Corpse be Interred in a private manner, without–parade, or funeral Oration.

Will of George Washington, 1799

tence of his valedictory letter to the governors of the states, written as he prepared to relinquish command of the Continental Army:

I now make it my earnest prayer, that God would have you, and the State over which you preside, in his holy protection, that he would incline the hearts of the Citizens to cultivate a spirit of subordination and obedience to Government, to entertain a brotherly affection and love for one another, for their fellow Citizens of the United States at large, and particularly for their brethren who have served in the Field, and finally, that he would most graciously be pleased to dispose us all, to do Justice, to love mercy, and to demean ourselves with that Charity, humility and pacific temper of mind, which were the Characteristicks of the Divine Author of our blessed Religion, and without an humble imitation of whose example in these things, we can never hope to be a happy Nation.

Immediately after Washington's death Congress resolved that a marble monument should be erected to his memory within the new Capitol in the city of Washington, and that his family should be requested to permit his body to be deposited beneath it. Mrs. Washington's consent was solicited and obtained. A crypt was provided under the dome of the Capitol, but the project was never completed, and the surviving executors finally (in 1831) removed the bodies of General and Mrs. Washington and those of other members of the family from the old vault to a similar structure within the present enclosure.

In 1832, when the nation observed the centennial of the birth of George Washington, the proposal for the removal of his body to the Capitol was revived. Congress authorized application to the proprietor of Mount Vernon, John A. Washington, for the transfer, but the legislature of the Commonwealth of Virginia requested him not to consent, and he elected to abide by the intent so implicit in the will of his great-uncle.

The marble sarcophagus in which the body of General Washington now rests was presented in 1837. At that time the leaden inner casket was removed from the closed vault to the new marble and permanently entombed within it. A similar sarcophagus, more plainly sculptured, was provided for the remains of Mrs. Washington.

The marble shafts in front of the Tomb were erected to the memory of Bushrod Washington and his nephew, John Augustine Washington, who in turn were proprietors of Mount Vernon. They are buried in the inner vault. The shafts at the side of the enclosure mark the graves of Nelly Custis Lewis and one of her daughters.

The family Vault at Mount Vernon requiring repairs, and being improperly situated besides, I desire that a new one of Brick, and upon a larger Scale, may be built at the foot of what is commonly called the Vineyard Inclosure, – on the ground which is marked out.
Will of George Washington, 1799

THE TREE-SHADED PATH TO THE SLAVE BURIAL GROUND AND MEMORIAL.

THE SLAVE BURIAL GROUND AND MEMORIAL

The Slave Burial Ground is identified as a cemetery used by slaves and free blacks in the eighteenth and nineteenth centuries. Ground penetrating radar indicates that as many as 75 graves may exist on this hillside overlooking the Potomac River. No markers survive to identify individuals buried in each grave, but records indicate that William Lee (c. 1750-1828), General Washington's personal servant during the Revolutionary War, is buried here. In 1929 the Mount Vernon Ladies' Association placed a stone marker at the Burial Ground to commemorate the site.

As a land-owner and planter in colonial Virginia, George Washington grew up in a world where slavery was part of the accepted order of things. Yet his attitude underwent a reversal over his lifetime, and he ultimately emancipated his slaves after his death. Many things contributed to the change. As Washington switched from tobacco to wheat and improved his farming operation, he needed a skilled work force and came to realize the drawbacks and poor economics of enslaved labor.

Leading the fight for liberty in the Revolution and his awareness of the principles of equality of the newly founded American nation influenced George Washington's thinking. He was also aware of the humanity and emotions of the slaves, especially their grief upon being separated from family and friends. About the time of the Revolution, he resolved never to purchase or sell a slave, later writing *I am principled against this kind of traffic in the human species...and to disperse the families I have an aversion.* Although Washington regarded slavery as legal and felt that the rights of slave owners were valid, by the end of his life he had concluded that slavery had no place in the American democracy, writing *I wish from my soul that the Legislature of this State could see the policy of a gradual Abolition of Slavery.*

Washington acted upon his belief by providing in his will for the emancipation of the slaves he owned. In July of 1799, as he prepared his will, Washington took a complete census of all slaves living at Mount Vernon. The census is particularly valuable because Washington recorded the ages, occupations, family relationships and legal ownership of every slave. Of the 316 slaves identified in the census, 123 were legally regarded as his. Forty slaves were rented from a neighbor, and the remaining 153 were "dower" slaves, part of the estate of Mrs. Washington's first husband, Daniel Parke Custis, and legally entailed to his heirs, her four grandchildren.

George Washington died five months after taking the census. His will provided for the immediate manumission of one slave, William Lee, *for his faithful services during the Revolutionary War.* His remaining slaves were to be freed at the end of Mrs. Washington's life, but she granted them freedom after one year. Washington's will established a *regular and permanent fund* for the care and support of the elderly and infirm among the newly freed people, and records show that his estate paid out pensions until 1833. Some continued to live at Mount Vernon for many years.

In 1983, a Slave Memorial was erected at the Slave Burial Ground, honoring those who served in slavery at Mount Vernon. The Memorial was designed by architecture students from Howard University in Washington, D.C., and features a granite memorial shaft in the center of a circular plaza. The low terraces around the shaft bear the words "hope," "love," and "faith," taken from the biblical scriptures that helped sustain African Americans while in slavery. The Slave Memorial is the focal point of an annual commemoration conducted by Black Women United for Action and the Mount Vernon Ladies' Association.

Washington's 1799 census of slaves, prepared as he made provisions in his will to emancipate those belonging to him.

108

IN MEMORY OF
THE AFRO AMERICANS
WHO SERVED AS SLAVES
AT MOUNT VERNON
THIS MONUMENT MARKING THEIR
BURIAL GROUND
DEDICATED
SEPTEMBER 21, 1983
MOUNT VERNON
LADIES' ASSOCIATION

THE CENTRAL MEMORIAL SHAFT OF THE SLAVE MEMORIAL

THE GARDENS AND GREENHOUSE

Over six acres are enclosed to create four separate gardens at Mount Vernon, and a greenhouse provides shelter for tropical exotics. The gardens served many purposes, from testing new varieties of plants, to producing vegetables and fruits, to providing lavish displays of beautiful flowers.

The gardens, the greenhouse, and the planted areas around the Mansion were the responsibility of a head gardener, who was usually an indentured servant or employee. Most of the gardeners were trained in Europe and "signed articles" to work for three or more years in exchange for an annual wage, housing, and in the case of John Ehlers, gardener from 1789 to 1797, passage from his home country of Germany. The gardener directed a work crew of as many as six slaves in caring for the landscape and gardens of Mount Vernon.

ABOVE: VIEW OF THE MANSION FROM THE GREENHOUSE.

FACING PAGE: THE UPPER GARDEN.

Tell the Gardener I shall expect everything that a Garden ought to produce, in the most ample manner.

Washington to William Pearce, June 5, 1796.

The upper garden is enclosed by brick walls and assumed its present size and shape in the mid-1780s, as Washington finished implementing his plan for the Mansion grounds. At the same time he planted the upper garden with flowers, removing the fruit and nut trees that originally grew here to create a colorful pleasure garden. Friends and neighbors contributed varieties such as crown imperial, cardinal flower, and guelder roses, and guests were soon delightedly exclaiming over the garden's "lilies, roses, and pinks," and enjoying the appearance and perfume of the flower displays. Interestingly, Washington rarely commented on the flowers that so impressed others, noting only a few varieties by name. Today the beds of the upper garden have been restored to their original locations, based on careful archaeological excavation, and are filled with annuals and perennials that were identified by visitors or known to have been grown in Virginia gardens of the period.

ABOVE: THE SEED HOUSE IN THE UPPER GARDEN.

FACING PAGE: THE FLOWER BEDS OF THE UPPER GARDEN.

It is miserable for a farmer to be obliged to buy his Seeds; to exchange Seeds may, in some cases, be useful; but to buy them after the first year is disreputable.
Washington to William Pearce, November 16, 1794

ABOVE: THE GREENHOUSE AND UPPER GARDEN IN WINTER.

FACING PAGE: NECESSARY IN THE LOWER GARDEN.

The gardener's weekly reports for 1798 report "digging and planting box edging" in the upper garden. Over the centuries these small English boxwoods have far outgrown their original beds, dominating many of the garden walks. Two boxwood parterres have been re-created, featuring the French fleur-de-lis design that Washington originally planted.

In 1785, George Washington built a large brick greenhouse fronting the upper garden on the north side. A visitor described it: "a complete Greenhouse which at this season is a vast, a great source of pleasure. Plants from ever part of the world seem to flourish in the neatly finished apartment, & from the arrangement of the whole, I conclude that it is managed by a skilful hand..." Washington soon filled the greenhouse with exotic orange and

None of the plants which were sowed with the seeds from China...were to be seen.
Washington's diary, 1786.

lemon trees, oleanders from the Carolinas, and sago palms from the West Indies. The same varieties are still grown at Mount Vernon, sheltered inside during the winter, and spending the warm months in the courtyard in front of the greenhouse. The greenhouse was destroyed by fire in 1835, and was reconstructed on the original foundation in 1951.

Just east of the upper garden, between it and the buildings on the north lane, is a modest botanical garden that was close to Washington's heart. This simple plot was largely tended by Washington himself, and used to test new and exotic plant varieties. His reputation as a keen plantsman prompted friends, foreign governments and even strangers to supply him with seeds, cuttings and bulb. These offerings usually received Washington's personal attention, as he would sow the seeds himself, care for the new sprouts, and record their ability to adapt to Virginia's soil and climate. Successes, such as the alfalfa and oats he first tested here, were quickly incorporated into his farming plan for Mount Vernon. Today the botanical garden is resown regularly to reflect Washington's experimental spirit.

THE VEGETABLE BEDS IN THE LOWER GARDEN

Plan of LOWER GARDEN

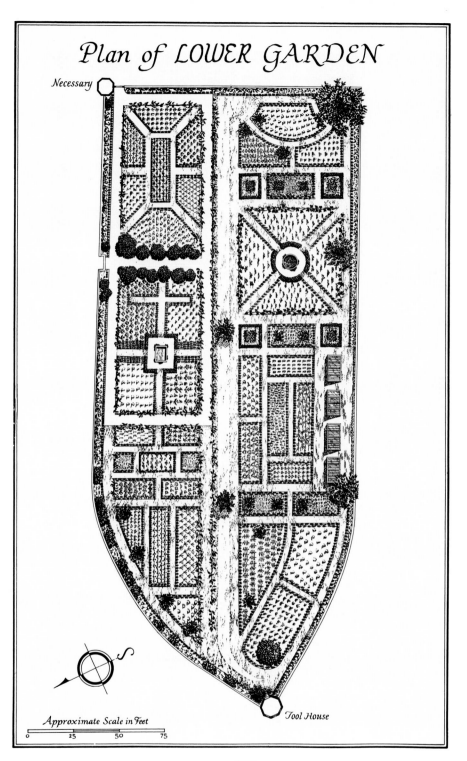

Necessary

Tool House

Approximate Scale in Feet

0   25   50   75

YOUNG TREES IN THE FRUIT GARDEN AND NURSERY

The kitchen garden is the same shape as the upper garden, and is symmetrically placed on the opposite side of the bowling green. The large English boxwoods that crowd the entrance walk were planted in 1786, possibly from cuttings sent by Light Horse Harry Lee. The kitchen garden drew little attention from visitors, and a rare description is taken from the diary of Julian Niemcewicz, a Polish visitor who was welcomed as a compatriot of Kosciusko, a Polish officer who joined the American cause in the Revolution. Niemcewicz spent twelve days at Mount Vernon in 1798: "In the evening G[eneral] Washington showed us round his garden. It is well cultivated, perfectly kept, and is quite in English style. All the vegetables indispensable for the kitchen were found there. Different kinds of berries—currants, raspberries, strawberries, gooseberries—a great quantity of peaches and cherries, but much inferior to ours..."

The plan of the restored kitchen garden is derived from the same books on gardening that were studied by George Washington. The vegetables, fruits, and herbs now grown in the garden are noted in his own writings and in the weekly reports of the gardener. The fruit trees, trained as espaliers against the garden wall and as cordons along the walks, are also noted in these records. The dipping cistern was a common feature of gardens, recommended in books of the time to expose and warm "..such Water as is taken of Wells, Etc." which otherwise was regarded as "by no Means proper for any Sort of Plants." Cold frames were used at Mount Vernon to give vegetables and annuals an early start in the spring.

The largest garden, the fruit garden and nursery, covers four acres just south of the stable. Washington first used this area to experiment with grapes, planting 2,000 grapevine cuttings here in 1771. The grapes were a casualty of the American Revolution, neglected and overgrown in his absence. Upon his return, Washington used the garden as a nursery, planting valuable varieties of grasses, wheat, grains, and vegetables to produce the volumes of seed needed to introduce these crops into the large-scale agriculture of his production farms. Washington also devoted two-thirds of the garden to an orchard, which supplied Mount Vernon's kitchen with plentiful fruit for many months of the year. He carefully recorded planting many varieties of pears, apples, peaches, and cherries, as well as unnamed varieties of plums and damsons.

While the fruit garden was protected with a strong post and rail fence, Washington sought to enclose it with a "live" fence, made of closely planted willow, poplar, locust, and hawthorne. His goal was to reduce the demand for lumber on his forests, while creating a permanent fence capable of turning away livestock, deer and other hungry wildlife. Today, the fruit garden and nursery has been carefully restored and replanted, based on archaeological evidence and Washington writings.

GEORGE WASHINGTON: PIONEER FARMER

George Washington became a farmer at age 22, when he first made Mount Vernon his home. As a new planter, Washington expected riches from tobacco, the crop that had made many of Virginia's landowners wealthy. But his hopes were never realized. Washington quickly recognized the shortcomings of traditional tobacco farming and began to seek improved ways of cultivating Mount Vernon's fields. As he tested new ideas and learned from his own experiences, he became a leader of the progressive farmers of his time. By the end of his life, Washington had succeeded in making Mount Vernon a successful farm, and in the process he had helped launch a revolution in American agriculture.

I begin my diurnal course with the Sun; if my hirelings are not in their places at that time I send them messages expressive of my sorrow for their indisposition; then having put these wheels in motion, I examine the state of things further; and the more they are probed, the deeper I find the wounds are which my buildings have sustained by an absence and neglect of eight years; by the time I have accomplished these matters, breakfast...is ready. This over, I mount my horse and ride around my farms, which employs me until it is time to dress for dinner.

Washington to James McHenry, May 29, 1797

Mount Vernon's land had been owned by the Washington family since 1674. It became George Washington's home in 1754, when he rented its 2,000 acres from the widow of his half-brother, Lawrence. At first, Washington directed his slave force—then numbering about twenty—to plant tobacco, as his half-brother and father had done before him. But Mount Vernon's fields were already exhausted by the crop, its nutrients depleted and its topsoil washed away by years of hoeing and shallow plowing. In addition, tobacco required a large labor force of slaves who were endlessly occupied in picking off worms and pests, hoeing out weeds, and pruning the plants to achieve a large leaf size. Finally, Washington realized that the market for tobacco was constantly changing and was controlled by agents in Britain. A planter could receive little or no income even with a good harvest.

As their plantation lands became worn out, many of Virginia's tobacco planters moved and cleared new tobacco fields in the west. George Washington determined he would make Mount Vernon profitable rather than move, and instead purchased adjoining farms, increasing Mount Vernon's acreage. He began experimenting with new crops, sowing small quantities of wheat, oats and rye and carefully monitoring which crop did

Above: Washington's reconstructed Gristmill, on Dogue Creek.

Facing page: An historic engraving, showing the wheat harvest at Mount Vernon.

121

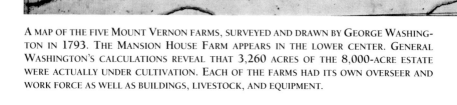

A MAP OF THE FIVE MOUNT VERNON FARMS, SURVEYED AND DRAWN BY GEORGE WASHINGTON IN 1793. THE MANSION HOUSE FARM APPEARS IN THE LOWER CENTER. GENERAL WASHINGTON'S CALCULATIONS REVEAL THAT 3,260 ACRES OF THE 8,000-ACRE ESTATE WERE ACTUALLY UNDER CULTIVATION. EACH OF THE FARMS HAD ITS OWN OVERSEER AND WORK FORCE AS WELL AS BUILDINGS, LIVESTOCK, AND EQUIPMENT.

Farm's and their Contents

Union Farm
Field Nº 1	120 acres
2	129
3	121
4	120
5	110
6	116
7	125
Meadow	42
	25 .. 67
Clover Lots	20	928

Muddy hole Farm
Field Nº 1	63
2	68
3	52
4	54
5	65
6	80
7	74
Clover Lots	20	476

Dogue R. Farm
Field Nº 1	70
2	74
3	74
4	71
5	75
6	73
7	80
Meadow	38
	18
	12
	10
	36 .. 114
Clover Lots	18	649

River Farm
Field Nº 1	120
2	120
3	125
4	132
5	132
6	130
7	120
Pasture	212
Orchards &c	84
Clover Lots	32	1207
Union Farm	928
Dogue Run Dº	649
In the 4 farm	3260

December 1793

others. — The greater of the
...red; and part still remains

...and in cultivation for a
...eat.

...ouse on it

...ub-divided, it might form part

W
E

Road to Alexandria 10 M.

E

Scale
100 200 300 400

E

Nº 7

Nº 5

Nº 4

River Farm

Nº 6

Orchard & Clover Lots

Clover Lots Clover Lots Clover Lots

Common Pasture

Nº 2

Nº 3

C

D

*The more I am acquainted with agricultural affairs the more I am pleased with them.
. . . I am led to reflect how much more delightful to an undebauched mind is the task of
making improvements on the earth, than all to vain glory which can be acquired from
ravaging it, by the most uninterrupted career of conquests.*
George Washington to Arthur Young, December 4, 1788

best. By 1767, he had abandoned tobacco and was planting Mount Vernon's fields in wheat and corn, foods that he could sell in Virginia as well as overseas. Washington constantly experimented with new crops to diversify his agricultural production, ultimately trying over 60 varieties at Mount Vernon. Washington also began expanding his farm operations, building a gristmill to process his grains and starting a fishery to harvest the plentiful fish in the Potomac River.

By the time Washington was selected to command the Continental Army in 1775, Mount Vernon was a thriving agricultural enterprise. It was largely self-sufficient, producing food for its owner and slave population, and wheat for sale and export. But General Washington was to be absent for eight years during the Revolutionary War. He attempted to direct his plantation through correspondence, but distance, war-time shortages and disruptions to shipping and markets took their toll.

As George Washington surveyed Mount Vernon after the Revolutionary War, he again needed to re-build his farms, and once more determined to improve his method of farming. His own experiences had taught him to place a high priority on careful management of the land, and he began to investigate ideas being developed in England, where the scarcity of land was forcing a reform of agriculture. By corresponding with leading farmers in England, Washington gained an understanding of this new approach, called the "New Husbandry," and resolved to pioneer this technique of farming in America.

Washington carefully tested the ideas of the New Husbandry, and was soon directing his overseers and slaves in practices that conserved the soil and reduced hand labor. He instituted deep plowing to reduce surface erosion and create a healthier root zone. He experimented with dozens of soil amendments and fertilizers, and selected creek mud, marl, manure, and

plaster of paris as ones which most improved his crops. He began planting in straight furrows laid out in regularly spaced rows rather than scatter seed across a tilled field. Instead of neglecting fallow land, he planted it in grasses and clover to restore its productivity. Washington became convinced that the traditional farming of his day was wasteful and misguided: *The present mode of cropping practised among us is destructive to landed property; and must, if persisted in much longer, ultimately ruin the holders of it.*

At the same time, Washington purchased several adjoining farms, expanding

ABOVE: OXEN PULLED PLOWS, HAULED TIMBER AND WATER, AND PROVIDED MANURE TO ENRICH MOUNT VERNON'S FIELDS.

FACING PAGE: INTERNS GATHER THE WHEAT HARVEST AT THE PIONEER FARMER SITE WITH REAP HOOKS AND SCYTHES.

Mount Vernon to an 8,000-acre plantation. He organized it into five units, the Mansion House Farm, and four working farms, River, Muddy Hole, Dogue and Union. Each working farm had its own overseer and work force of slaves, homes and cabins, livestock, fields, barns, and equipment. To accommodate another innovation, rotating crops on a seven-year cycle, Washington laid out seven fields at all of the four working farms. His crop rotation scheme favored the land more than his pocket book, producing a saleable crop in only three of the seven years. Washington explained this approach to a newly hired farm manager: *I know full well that by picking and culling the fields I should be able, for a year or two, to make large crops of grain; but I know also, that by so doing I shall, in a few years make nothing, and find my land ruined.* Washington was seeking to farm in a way that produced a steady income year after year, without wearing out the land.

Washington made similar advances in the equipment used in his fields. He sought to substitute horse-pulled implements for hand tools, and used plows, harrows, and cultivators not only to break up the ground but also to prepare the soil for planting and to remove weeds between rows. Washington designed a new plow, invented a clover stripper, constructed a "spikey roller" to till his fields, and adapted a barrel as a seeder, designing it to drop seed at regular intervals in a straight line as it was rolled down a row. Washington integrated his livestock into his farming, fattening the animals

THE SOLE SURVIVING PHOTOGRAPH OF WASHINGTON'S INNOVATIVE 16-SIDED TREADING BARN.
THE BARN IS BELIEVED TO HAVE BEEN DEMOLISHED SOMETIME AFTER 1870.

on grass and clover grown in fallow fields, and using their manure as a valuable enrichment for the soil. After careful study, he concluded that mules, the offspring of a mare and a jackass, would be a hardworking, economical farm animal, and used his prestige to import male jackasses from Spain. Mules proved their worth, and within a dozen years 105 of his working horses were replaced by 58 mules. Mules soon became the work animal of choice not only at Mount Vernon, but on farms across America.

Accompanying these changes in the fields, Washington embarked on an ambitious program to improve the handling of his harvest by constructing better farm buildings. Writing to prominent English agriculturalist Arthur Young in 1786, Washington requested a plan of *the most complete and useful farm-yard*, including a barn. Washington followed this plan in building a large, rectangular brick barn in 1789. With its huge size, the barn could accommodate indoor wheat threshing—normally a task conducted outdoors to provide room for the swinging flails used to beat the wheat stalks until the grain was knocked out of the straw. But his departure for the presidency that year left Washington struggling to direct these changes through correspondence with his farm manager. When he visited Mount

I think with you that the life of a Husbandman of all others is the most delectable. It is honorable. It is amusing, and, with judicious management, it is profitable.
Washington to Alexander Spotswood, February 3, 1788

Vernon the next year, he discovered the slaves still threshing on the bare ground, and now directing horses to tread on the wheat to break out the grain.

Determined to get threshing under cover to reduce loss and keep the wheat clean and safe from weather, Washington invented a new type of treading barn. His design had 16 sides, making it nearly round, perfectly shaped for horses or mules walking in a circle. Its massive timbers were strong enough to support livestock treading on the second floor, and a slatted floor permitted the grain to fall through to the level below. The grain was collected on the lower floor, winnowed in dutch fans and baskets, and stored in central bins. The brick walls and barred windows of the lower floor provided security against theft. The straw left behind on the upper

THE OX CART RETURNS TO THE FIELDS AFTER ITS LOAD OF WHEAT HAS BEEN SPREAD IN THE RECONSTRUCTED TREADING BARN.

floor was gathered and used in stables or for composting. The barn was built partly in an embankment, creating a gently-sloped entrance to the second floor for livestock.

Thanks to a generous grant from the W. K. Kellogg Foundation, Washington's remarkable 16-sided *treading house* has been reconstructed at Mount Vernon on a four-acre site near the Potomac River. The barn exactly follows Washington's plans and drawings from the 1790s, and the adjoining stables and corn houses are part of Washington's design. Every building was made of hand-shaped bricks, lumber hewed and pit-sawed to final dimension and nails hammered at an open-fire forge. In season, horses and mules tread wheat on the upper floor of the treading barn, just as happened under Washington's direction. In the adjoining fields, visitors are welcome to walk among the crops that make up one of Washington's seven year crop

127

rotations, examine the fertilizers he used, and see first-hand the farming techniques that Washington used to overcome the challenges of farming at Mount Vernon.

About the same time, Washington modernized and expanded his gristmill. He purchased plans from a young inventor, Oliver Evans, and used them to convert his mill into one of the most advanced water-powered mills available. Evans' design used the motion of the turning water wheel to power not only the grinding stones but also a complex system of conveyor belts and chutes to move the grain, and processing equipment such as a flour sifter and hopper boy. The result was an automated mill that that could often be operated by one man. With two sets of grindstones, one of fine French limestone for wheat, the other for corn, Washington milled grain for farmers throughout the area, taking the customary one-eighth of the produce in payment. Washington also carefully watched market prices and would sell his wheat as either grain or flour, whichever brought the highest price.

George Washington also expanded the mill complex to include a cooperage for making barrels and a large-scale distillery, which converted his grains into valuable whiskey. The mill enterprises were operated by as many as eleven slaves. A reconstruction of Washington's gristmill, a property owned by the Commonwealth of Virginia, has been restored to operating condition by a partnership between Virginia and Mount Vernon, and will open for visitation in the year 2000.

To a friend George Washington wrote: *my agricultural pursuits and rural amusements...ha[ve] been the most pleasing occupation of my life, and the most congenial to my temper, notwithstanding that a small proportion of it has been spent in this way.* Despite the demands of his public career, and his achievements in winning the Revolution and establishing the new American nation as first president, Washington thought of himself, first and foremost, as a farmer.

George Washington's new Mount Vernon was more productive, yet required less field labor. Just as Washington was a military and national leader, he had became a leader in agriculture. Many poorer American farmers could neither study about nor risk experimenting with new ways of farming. By helping perfect these techniques and demonstrate their success, Washington hoped to persuade others to adopt improved ways of farming. Equally important, Washington helped pioneer the use of scientific method in agriculture. He had shown that new ideas could be tested through careful experiments and that every aspect of farming could be analyzed and improved, bringing about America's first agricultural revolution. He envisioned America becoming having the strength and resources to be a world leader, and *a storehouse and granary for the world.*

THE STABLES, CORNHOUSES, AND BARNYARD THAT WASHINGTON DESIGNED AS PART OF THE TREADING BARN COMPLEX.

THE FOREST TRAIL

Well over half of Mount Vernon's 8,000 acres were not cultivated, and Washington left most of that in natural woodlands. These forests supplied firewood for the estate's entire population, lumber for countless buildings and barns, posts and rails for fences, and wild game for the table. Washington emphasized the importance of conserving the forest trees in

THE FOREST TRAIL WINDS THROUGH THE WOODLANDS OF MOUNT VERNON AND CULMINATES IN A SOARING FOOTBRIDGE OVER A DEEP RAVINE.

letters to his farm managers, and protected wildlife by prohibiting hunters from stalking deer on his land.

Visitors to the forest trail discover these peaceful yet vital woodlands, and learn of the changes that time and man have made in the make-up of the plant and animal community in the Virginia countryside.

MOUNT VERNON IS STILL HOME TO WILD TURKEYS, DEER AND OTHER WILDLIFE THAT ARE OFTEN GLIMPSED OR HEARD IN THE WOODS.

MARTHA WASHINGTON'S FAN

THE MOUNT VERNON MUSEUM

The Mount Vernon Museum is a modern structure, designed to be compatible with the original buildings. It was erected in 1928 to house the growing collection of objects and artifacts related to the lives of General and Mrs. Washington. Now it is used as a unique display space, to make accessible some of the most important and treasured objects related to the Washingtons, and to present special exhibitions on historic topics and themes.

The bust of George Washington was modeled at Mount Vernon in 1785 by the French sculptor, Jean Antoine Houdon. While in Paris, Houdon was engaged by Thomas Jefferson on behalf of the Commonwealth of Virginia, and asked to create a statue of the state's first citizen. Houdon arrived at Mount Vernon with three assistants in October 1785. After a careful study that included casting a plaster mask of Washington's face, Houdon modeled this likeness in clay as his first model. According to traditions, the clay

When the Mount Vernon Ladies' Association acquired Mount Vernon in 1858, the Mansion was empty of almost all furnishings and objects. In the years since, the Association has sought to recover original furnishings and personal possessions of the Washingtons to return Mount Vernon to its appearance in 1799, the last year of General Washington's life. Many items have been generously donated or loaned by collectors and family descendants to benefit the visiting public.

GEORGE WASHINGTON'S DRESSING CASE

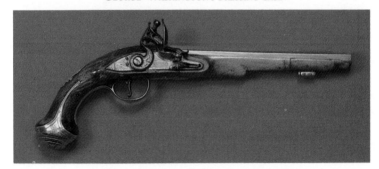

ONE OF A PAIR OF PISTOLS MADE BY WOOLEY

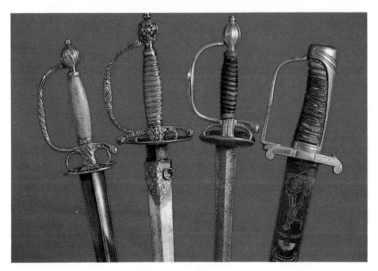

WASHINGTON'S SWORDS

TEAPOT FROM WASHINGTON'S CINCINNATI SERVICE AND A COVERED CUP WITH
SAUCER FROM MARTHA WASHINGTON'S "STATES" TEA SERVICE

CHINESE EXPORT MEAT DISH, ONE OF MANY IN THE POPULAR BLUE AND WHITE
PATTERNS USED AT MOUNT VERNON THROUGHOUT THE YEARS

MILK JUG, COFFEE CUP, AND SAUCER FROM THE NIDERVILLER SERVICE, GIVEN TO WASHINGTON BY THE COMTE DE CUSTINE IN 1782

DETAIL OF A SAUCER FROM THE "STATES" SERVICE, IN WHICH THE NAMES OF FIFTEEN STATES FORM A LINKED BORDER WITH MRS. WASHINGTON'S INITIALS IN THE SUNBURST

sculpture was fired in the bake oven in Mount Vernon's kitchen. Houdon made plaster impressions of the clay bust for use in completing the statue after returning to Paris. The bust remained at Mount Vernon and John A. Washington, Jr., the last private owner of the estate, presented it to the Mount Vernon Ladies' Association upon its purchase of Mount Vernon. Houdon's completed statue, a full-length, standing figure of George Washington carved in marble, is on display in the rotunda of the Virginia state Capitol in Richmond. Houdon's sculpture was created when Washington was 53, and was regarded by members of his household as the best of all the likenesses made of him.

In his will, General Washington bequeathed swords to five nephews with the stirring injunction that they *were not to unsheath them for the purpose of shedding blood, except it be for self defence, or in defence of their Country and its rights; and in the latter case, to keep them unsheathed, and prefer falling with them in their hands, to the relinquishment thereof.* Swords chosen by three of the nephews under this provision and a fourth, which also belonged to Washington, are part of the Mount Vernon Museum collection.

Many military items are in the collection, such as pistols used by General Washington during the Revolution, portions of his military uniform, including saddlebags, and a telescope. The collection also includes a sash that was presented to Washington by General Braddock, as Braddock lay mortally wounded after the fatal ambush at Big Meadows in 1755, one of the opening battles of the French and Indian War.

GEORGE WASHINGTON
BY WALTER ROBERTSON, 1794

MARTHA WASHINGTON
BY JAMES PEALE, 1796

Objects of a more domestic nature are also represented. The Washingtons owned and used five principal sets of china, including blue and white Chinese export that was in "common use" at Mount Vernon. The "States" set of china featured the initials of Mrs. Washington and a border made of the names of the fifteen states that comprised the American nation at the end of Washington's presidency. The Cincinnati service was decorated with the eagle insignia of the Society of the Cincinnati, an organization of the officers who served in the Continental Army or Navy. General Washington served as the first President-General of the Society. Other important pieces from the Washington household include bisque table decorations and pieces of Washington and Custis silver, some of which are on loan through the generosity of a descendant of Mrs. Washington.

Personal items of the Washingtons' are also in the collection. Objects used by Mrs. Washington include some of her finest jewelry, fine fans, gloves, sewing implements and chair cushions she cross-stitched. Personal items of General Washington's include sunglasses, surveying instruments, dental tools, and clothing. Many of these objects can be displayed only for short periods of time, to ensure their preservation for future generations.

Miniature portraits form an important part of the collection. Two members of the artistic Peale family, Charles Willson and his brother James, created miniatures of Mrs. Washington. Charles Willson Peale also painted rare portraits of her two children by her first marriage, Martha Parke Custis and John Parke Custis, both of whom died at a young age.

MARTHA PARKE CUSTIS
BY CHARLES WILLSON PEALE, 1772

JOHN PARKE CUSTIS
BY CHARLES WILLSON PEALE, 1772

SILVER COFFEEPOT ENGRAVED WITH WASHINGTON'S
COAT-OF-ARMS, MADE IN PHILADELPHIA IN 1783
BY JOSEPH ANTHONY

CHAIR CUSHION, ONE OF TWELVE, WORKED IN CROSS-STITCH BY
MARTHA WASHINGTON OVER A PERIOD OF THIRTY-SIX YEARS

ONE OF SIX LEATHER
FIREBUCKETS MADE
IN PHILADELPHIA FOR
MOUNT VERNON

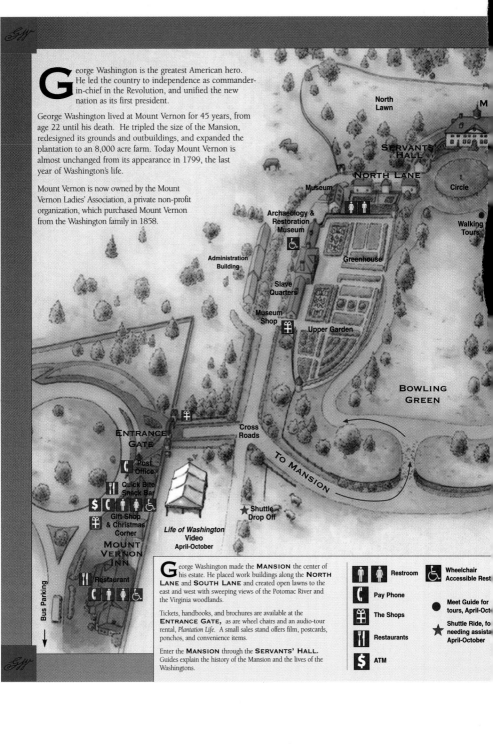

George Washington is the greatest American hero. He led the country to independence as commander-in-chief in the Revolution, and unified the new nation as its first president.

George Washington lived at Mount Vernon for 45 years, from age 22 until his death. He tripled the size of the Mansion, redesigned its grounds and outbuildings, and expanded the plantation to an 8,000 acre farm. Today Mount Vernon is almost unchanged from its appearance in 1799, the last year of Washington's life.

Mount Vernon is now owned by the Mount Vernon Ladies' Association, a private non-profit organization, which purchased Mount Vernon from the Washington family in 1858.

North Lawn

M

SERVANTS' HALL

NORTH LANE

Circle

Museum

Walking Tours

Archaeology & Restoration Museum

Administration Building

Greenhouse

Slave Quarters

Museum Shop

Upper Garden

BOWLING GREEN

ENTRANCE GATE

Cross Roads

TO MANSION

Post Office

Quick Bite Snack Bar

Gift Shop & Christmas Corner

MOUNT VERNON INN

Shuttle Drop Off

Life of Washington Video April-October

Bus Parking

Restaurant

George Washington made the **MANSION** the center of his estate. He placed work buildings along the **NORTH LANE** and **SOUTH LANE** and created open lawns to the east and west with sweeping views of the Potomac River and the Virginia woodlands.

Tickets, handbooks, and brochures are available at the **ENTRANCE GATE,** as are wheel chairs and an audio-tour rental, *Plantation Life.* A small sales stand offers film, postcards, ponchos, and convenience items.

Enter the **MANSION** through the **SERVANTS' HALL.** Guides explain the history of the Mansion and the lives of the Washingtons.

Restroom

Wheelchair Accessible Rest

Pay Phone

Meet Guide for tours, April-Oct

The Shops

Shuttle Ride, fo needing assista April-October

Restaurants

ATM

A Brief Washington–Custis Genealogy

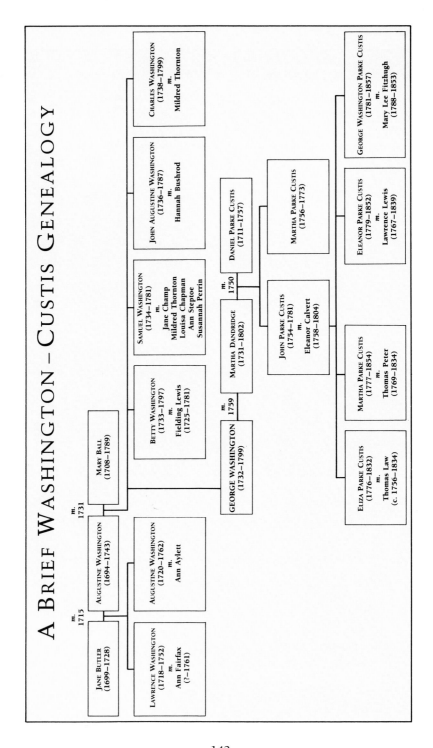

Jane Butler
(1699–1728)

m.
1715

Augustine Washington
(1694–1743)

Mary Ball
(1708–1789)

m.
1731

Lawrence Washington
(1718–1752)
m.
Ann Fairfax
(?–1761)

Augustine Washington
(1720–1762)
m.
Ann Aylett

Betty Washington
(1733–1797)
m.
Fielding Lewis
(1725–1781)

Samuel Washington
(1734–1781)
m.
Jane Champ
Mildred Thornton
Louisa Chapman
Ann Steptoe
Susannah Perrin

John Augustine Washington
(1736–1787)
m.
Hannah Bushrod

Charles Washington
(1738–1799)
m.
Mildred Thornton

George Washington
(1732–1799)

m.
1759

Martha Dandridge
(1731–1802)

m.
1750

Daniel Parke Custis
(1711–1757)

Eliza Parke Custis
(1776–1832)
m.
Thomas Law
(c. 1756–1834)

Martha Parke Custis
(1777–1854)
m.
Thomas Peter
(1769–1834)

John Parke Custis
(1754–1781)
m.
Eleanor Calvert
(1758–1804)

Martha Parke Custis
(1756–1773)

Eleanor Parke Custis
(1779–1852)
m.
Lawrence Lewis
(1767–1839)

George Washington Parke Custis
(1781–1857)
m.
Mary Lee Fitzhugh
(1788–1853)

THE
MOUNT VERNON
LADIES'
ASSOCIATION
OF THE UNION

ANN PAMELA CUNNINGHAM

After the death of George and Martha Washington, Mount Vernon remained in the Washington family for three generations. But inheritance reduced the estate's vast acreage, changing markets made its agricultural products unprofitable, and curiosity brought increasing numbers of visitors. The last Washington owner, John Augustine Washington, Jr., a great-great nephew of George Washington, found his position untenable, and he tried to interest both the federal government and the state of Virginia in acquiring the historic home. Both governments refused.

Learning of this, Ann Pamela Cunningham of South Carolina resolved to preserve Mount Vernon as a national shrine. She founded the Mount Vernon Ladies' Association in 1853, recruiting women from other states to raise money for the cause. In December, 1858, Miss Cunningham and her ladies were able to purchase the Mansion and 200 acres of surrounding land for $200,000. Restoration began immediately and the estate opened to the public. Since that time, the Association has devoted itself to restoring and furnishing Mount Vernon as it was in 1799, the last year of Washington's life. The Association also encourages education about the life and legacy of George Washington.

The Association's board still consists of trustees, or Vice Regents, who represent their home states, and an elected Regent, or chairman. The Association operates as a non-profit organization under a charter from the Commonwealth of Virginia, holding Mount Vernon as a public trust. The Association operates without financial assistance from state or federal governments, and is funded entirely by admission fees, sales revenues, and donations from patriotic foundations, businesses and individuals.

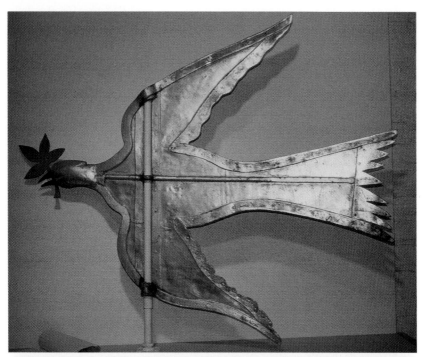

THE ARCHAEOLOGY AND RESTORATION MUSEUM

The Archaeology and Restoration Museum features the ongoing efforts of the Mount Vernon Ladies' Association to restore and maintain Mount Vernon and discover more about its historic residents. Here you will see some of the tools and techniques that Washington's skilled craftsmen used in the construction of the Mansion, and the care that their modern counterparts take to preserve and replicate their workmanship. Some original items are displayed here, such as the dove of peace weathervane, removed from the Mansion's cupola to protect it from the elements.

An extensive archaeology program has slowly unearthed many secrets about Mount Vernon. Excavations of slave living areas have provided clues about their diet, material possessions, and activities, while a Mansion trash pit has yielded important artifacts relating to the Washingtons. Archaeology is also used to identify the location and purpose of long-vanished work buildings, and helps determine the exact appearance of Mount Vernon in Washington's time.

ABOVE: BOTH THE WHITE, SALTGLAZED STONEWARE BOWL ON THE LEFT AND THE HAND-MADE, UNGLAZED COLONO-WARE BOWL ON THE RIGHT WERE USED BY SLAVES AT MOUNT VERNON AND EXCAVATED FROM THE CELLAR OF THE HOUSE FOR FAMILIES.

FACING PAGE TOP: THE DOVE OF PEACE WEATHERVANE, ACQUIRED BY WASHINGTON IN 1787 FOR INSTALLATION ON THE MANSION CUPOLA AT MOUNT VERNON.

FACING PAGE BOTTOM: A TRASHPIT JUST SOUTH OF THE MANSION YIELDED RARE ARTIFACTS FROM THE 1760S, INCLUDING THESE TOY FIGURES, WHICH WERE PROBABLY PLAYTHINGS OF MRS. WASHINGTON'S YOUNG CHILDREN.

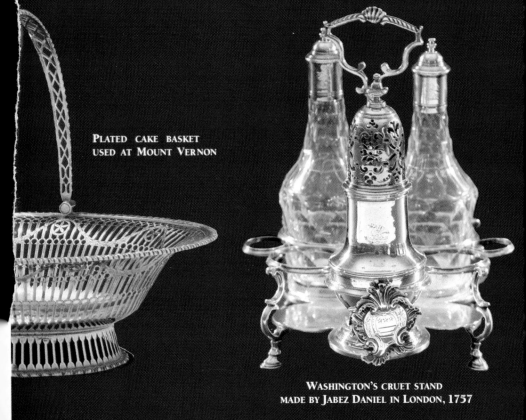

PLATED CAKE BASKET
USED AT MOUNT VERNON

WASHINGTON'S CRUET STAND
MADE BY JABEZ DANIEL IN LONDON, 1757

MARTHA WASHINGTON'S GOLD NECKLACE SURROUNDS A SMALL COLLECTION OF HER JEWELRY,
A GARNET STICKPIN, GOLD LOOPS, AND ENAMEL RING WITH PEARL